A Framework for Physical Education in the Early Years

A Framework for Physical Education in the Early Years

by

Hazel Kathleen Manners
and Margaret E. Carroll

The Falmer Press

(A member of the Taylor & Francis Group)
London • Washington, D.C.

UK   The Falmer Press, 4 John Street, London WC1N 2ET
USA   The Falmer Press, Taylor & Francis Inc., 1900 Frost Road, Suite 101, Bristol, PA 19007

First published in 1995

A catalogue record for this book is available from the British Library

Library of Congress Cataloging-in-Publication Data are available on request

ISBN 0 7507 0417 9 paper

Typeset in 10/12 pt Garamond and printed by
Graphicraft Typesetters Ltd., Hong Kong.

Contents

Acknowledgments

Photographs: Les Cross, University of Brighton Children from Bevendean Primary School, Brighton and St Mary Magdalen Roman Catholic School, Hove.

Physical Education Non Statutory Guidance (*Section E1*), NCC, 1992, Crown copyright is reproduced with the permission of the Controller of HMSO.

Preface

This book endeavours to cover a comprehensive look at National Curriculum physical education to Key Stage 1. Six basic principles are identified which provide the foundation for the rationale, curriculum content, teaching and planning processes required in providing a balanced programme for children between the ages of 3 and 7. A bank of ideas for warming up and calming down activities that can be used in lessons is also included.

Concise explanations of some of the terms used in physical education will help clarify technical phraseology which is often confusing to the non-specialist.

Special attention is paid to movement education in the nursery, an important area of physical activity which can lead on to the work that will be introduced in the reception classes. Games, gymnastic activities, dance and swimming are covered in detail and two sample units of work for each age group provide students in training and teachers with valuable material for use in schools. All the material provided has been tried and tested in schools by both students and practising infant teachers.

The final chapter looks at the role of the curriculum leader or coordinator for physical education at Key Stage 1 offering advice on how to agree and implement a common school policy with OFSTED inspections in mind.

It is not intended that this book should be read from cover to cover, but as a reference book to which students involved in initial teacher training and class teachers can go for help and ideas. Therefore in certain instances there is an element of repetition especially where important factors such as safety need to be stressed. In order to make the reading of the text simple and fluent, the word 'she' is used when referring to the teacher and the word 'he' refers to the child.

Introduction

'Where there is life there is movement; where there are children there is almost perpetual movement. Children normally run, jump, throw, catch, kick, strike, and perform a multitude of basic skills.' (Wickstrom, 1970)

If we are to consider the development of the whole child, then we cannot exclude physical development. Children learn through doing whether it be counting, painting, talking, building or climbing, swinging and jumping. No one would deny the importance of physical activity and any parent will recognize the child's capacity to 'keep on the go'.

There is real concern that children of today are not getting enough exercise (Sleap and Warburton, 1990) and a structured programme of physical activity in which real learning is taking place is of paramount importance.

'Several studies suggest that primary schools are devoting only 3 per cent of curriculum time to PE on average — rather than the recommended 5 per cent.' (*Times Educational Supplement*, March 1994)

An NAHT/CCPR report in 1992 showed that primary schools in the UK were bottom of the list in the amount of time devoted to physical education in primary schools, the list comprising all the major European countries. Five out of the nine countries listed devoted more than twice the time to physical education than the UK. Added to this only 8 per cent of all primary teachers have received training in physical education over and above the basic professional course. The amount of time allocated to physical education in initial teacher training is repeatedly being cut to accommodate extra time spent on the core subjects. Changes to teacher training as a result of the recommendations made in the Government document *Circular 14/93* will have profound effects on the way teachers are trained and physical education may suffer badly in the long run as a result.

The arguments for class teachers to teach physical education rather than so called physical education 'specialists' in the early years is very strong. If we regard physical education as being 'education through the physical' then education principles apply wherever the educating is taking place. Good class teachers will use their classroom strategies in physical education just as they do in the classroom but there is the added dimension of the children being 'on the move' and this calls for extra vigilance regarding safety, coping with social factors such as sharing and turn taking, and helping children to handle competition.

The lesson time should be structured so that it is not wasted and the children kept active for as much of the time as possible. Timetabled lessons should not be sacrificed for other events, or if this is inevitable, then the time should be made up so that at least the minimum recommendation of thirty-six hours during the school year is maintained.

There are two unique features of PE. One is its physicality and therefore its transience and the other is that in many cases the child is able to perform better than the teacher!

At the end of the school day, the child is able to show evidence of many of his activities, his painting, his model, his sums, but what evidence has he of his PE? This presents problems for the teacher; she must remember what each child did and cannot rely on tangible results, nor can she refer to the evidence produced by other teachers. She can go into the classroom next door at playtime and say, 'Those children's models look interesting, how did the children make them?' Very seldom does she have the opportunity to see another class and its teacher in action in the hall.

> 'The paradox with which we are faced is that while it is the physical nature of the subject which gives it its distinct identity and its unique place in the curriculum, it is this very physical nature which places it at the periphery of the curriculum.' (Williams, 1989)

Most children are very agile, supple, strong, fearless and inventive. In the classroom the child is struggling to make sense of the adult world, dominated by signs and symbols that he has ultimately to master. This is not the case in physical activities. By the age of 7 the child will be able to do all the basic actions, although he will be struggling with coordination, balance, control and the application of these actions for many years to come.

National Curriculum Physical Education

The National Curriculum Physical Education Order outlines the programmes of study for each area of activity, i.e. games, gymnastic activities, dance and swimming (optional) for Key Stage 1. It does not introduce anything new but puts into focus all the good teaching in physical education that has been going on since the 1970s. We should not be planning anything revolutionary, instead we should be using the National Curriculum statements to check that we give our children a balanced programme, resulting in their becoming skilful, knowledgeable and eager to do more.

The difference is that since its conception, National Curriculum Physical Education gives the subject recognition and credence. Now that it is statutory it should reverse the decline in time allocated to the subject and improve the importance put on it, not least by the children themselves.

Chapter One

Principles on Which Physical Education Between the Ages of 3 and 7 Depend

There are six principles on which the teaching of physical education between the ages of 3 and 7 depend:

(i) physical education builds on what the child can already do;

(ii) children should be as active as possible during physical education;

(iii) lessons should be regarded as learning situations with clear, structured outcomes identified;

(iv) there should be a range of activities and sufficient time given to the subject;

(v) in order to achieve a balanced programme there should be sufficient equipment and adequate facilities;

(vi) all children are entitled to the best physical education programme possible.

Principle 1: Physical education builds on what the child can already do

A baby uses movement in a variety of ways, not only to explore his surroundings and to investigate attractive objects within his grasp but also to gain responses from his mother, father and other adults.

A child of 6 months left lying on his back will roll over onto his tummy to reach a toy; in his pram he will throw out his rattle over and over again in order to elicit a response from an adult

in a game-like way. Lying in a prone position he pushes himself up on his arms and later when on his hands and knees he rocks forwards and backwards prior to crawling. Once mobile on his feet he runs playfully away from his mother, enjoying the chase and the thrill of being caught up in her arms.

By the age of 3 the child seldom walks sedately anywhere but skips, hops, runs and jumps, often repeating a little jumpy pattern. He expresses sheer exuberance of the joy of being alive. Every little wall he comes to he persistently wants to climb on and every gate is a swing.

Adults feed in verbal commands such as, 'Come and put your coat on'; 'Go and fetch Teddy', to which he responds physically. To compensate for his lack of appropriate speech to make himself understood, a 2-year-old will hold up a sore thumb for sympathetic inspection conveying meaning through his actions and gestures.

Thus the basic actions of rolling, rocking, climbing, running, jumping, swinging and throwing are fully explored by the time the child reaches school age. He uses these in a very purposeful way, namely to:

get somewhere, to reach something;
play a game;
express his feelings;
explore rhythms and patterns;
learn about communication and language;
act out role plays of his own devising,

entering into his own little world of fantasy and imagination.

This principle, then, is our starting point.

By the age of 5 a child will be broadening his horizon; he is ready to play alongside and with other children and can start to master skills such as catching a ball, learning to skip with a rope, jump and land safely from a low box or table, swing on a rope.

At 6 the child should be able to cooperate with a partner, understand and make up simple rules in a game, and follow a simple pattern of jumping and hopping actions.

On leaving the infant school the child ought to be able to catch and throw a ball with a degree of accuracy, bounce a ball using a play bat, run well, roll, balance and jump with confidence and play simple games involving three or four children. He will be capable of exploring movement in an expressive way through the medium of dance-like actions lacking inhibition or self-consciousness and will enjoy making up dances with other children providing he understands very basic choreographic forms.

These are all outlined in the National Curriculum Physical Education statutory orders in the 'End of Key Stage' descriptions, namely:

Key Stage 1

'Pupils, plan and perform simple skills safely, and show control in linking actions together. They improve their performance through practising their skills, working alone and with a partner. They talk about what they have done and are able to make simple judgements. They recognise and describe the changes that happen to their bodies during exercise.'

Principle 2: Children should be as active as possible during physical education

To most people it would seem obvious that this is the case but research has shown that children can be active for less than three minutes in a thirty-minute lesson. Time is taken up for getting changed, putting out equipment, listening to instructions and watching demonstrations, all of which, teachers will argue, are important learning situations for the children, but those concerned with the health of our children want vigorous activity that will increase the heart rate and make and keep our children fit.

Although a great deal of research has been done in America, there is not much actual evidence to prove what we suspect, i.e. that our children are not as fit as those in previous generations. This is partly due to the fact that it is difficult to apply fitness tests to young children and activity is not the same as fitness, other factors such as motivation having to be taken into consideration. This will be explained in more detail later. We know too that children, on average, spend three hours a day watching television.

The 'Happy Heart Project' which looked at physical activity patterns of primary school children aged between 5 and 11, found that:

- '8 to 11-year-olds were generally more active than 4 to 7-year-olds;
- a quarter of children's free time was spent watching television;
- a quarter of all PE lessons was spent standing still or sitting;
- overall children engaged in very little physical activity.' (Sleap, Perch and Warburton, 1990)

Therefore we have to examine our practice and endeavour to improve the quality of both the learning and the doing.

Time taken up getting the children changed can be curtailed, maybe by introducing an egg-timer to motivate them, getting the slower children changed before the others so the quick ones are not left ready and waiting by the door for longer than necessary. Do the children need to get changed for every activity? Is it realistic for them to strip down to vest and pants to go outside for a games lesson and then later be told to put their coats on to go outside at play-time? Could the uniform be changed to avoid the hassle of doing up ties and tiny shirt buttons?

How can setting out the large apparatus be organized safely and efficiently? Does it all need to be set out in advance so the hall looks like a jungle gym, or does the activity require a few simple boxes and mats that the children can easily move into place themselves? Is the apparatus readily available around the sides of the room or is it bundled away in a cupboard along with the overhead projector, props for the Christmas play and sacks of secondhand clothes ready for the school jumble sale?

Tasks which we set the children need to be simple enough for them to respond immediately and actively without lengthy explanations and demonstrations. Do we as teachers circulate, encouraging, praising, demanding quality and effort, actively participating rather than passively standing in one place watching the children to make sure they work in complete silence?

How can we avoid long queues of children waiting for a 'go' on the ropes, are there enough balls for everyone to play with? Is the game one in which they are all involved or are some waiting for turns? Elimination games are not suitable for infants especially as the child most likely to be eliminated first is the one who needs the most practice thus losing all chance of improving whilst the 'best' has the most opportunity to practise. In what other area of the curriculum do we eliminate children? Do we, for example, exclude children who get their sums wrong? In the same vein relay races are non-productive for infants as the child waiting for his turn probably only sees the back view of the child in front of him whilst waiting.

The nature of the activities will demand different responses from the children and the teacher can identify which lessons can be more 'action-packed' than others, bearing in mind this principle and thus making sure that whenever the opportunity arises our children are as active as possible in a safe, constructive manner.

Principle 3: Lessons should be regarded as learning situations with clear, structured outcomes identified

Careful planning is necessary just as much in physical education as any other curriculum area. Local authorities often produce detailed guidelines and schools have their own documents, but teachers need to be involved in the overall planning in order to feel they have 'ownership' of the materials produced and willing to improve the quality of their teaching where necessary.

All infant teachers will recognize the need for routine procedures with young children and lessons should follow a similar pattern where possible.

'Children learn most from activities with a clear goal.' (Sylva and Lundt 1982)

Some physical education activities will be of an exploratory nature. Reception children may be given a range of games equipment to select from and play with; Year 2 children may have an arrangement of large apparatus in gymnastics on which to work out a movement phrase based on a specific task.

The teacher should be clear about why she has chosen a particular activity and what she wants the children to achieve, similarly the children need to understand what they are doing and why.

Having mastered an activity the time has come to move on to another activity or apply the activity to a different situation so the teacher keeps challenging the children and demanding more from them.

Tasks set for the children can be open-ended, i.e. 'find a way of . . .' allowing for differentiation and encouraging imaginative and individual responses, or they can be directed, for example, 'hop round the room on one leg'. The tasks can be specifically challenging to the children, for example, 'can you knock a skittle over by rolling a football along the ground with your hands?'

The way the task is presented to the children

will depend on the outcome the teacher wants. She needs to be clear in her own mind not only what she is expecting from the children but how to formulate successive tasks depending on the response. This requires acute observation both of the class as a whole and individual children in the class. If for example, the task, 'find a way of balancing on one hand and one foot' produces a rather stereotyped response from the class as a whole she will then have to feed in suggestions, such as, 'try balancing face upwards' or, 'stretch out sideways as you balance'; she can select children who have responded differently and use them to demonstrate to the others to give them some ideas. Discussion with the children on other ways of balancing on one hand and one foot may elicit more individual responses.

If the task set is skill oriented, i.e. one in which the outcome is a recognized form such as catching a ball, the teacher will look for individual achievement and identify those finding the task difficult. She will need to recognize the problem, failing to watch the ball for example, and decide whether to break down the skill or just give a verbal piece of advice, taking into consideration all the factors that influence the child's personal ability, his strength, sense of timing, motivation, concentration, coordination etc.

Children mainly learn through doing. So whilst they are working the teacher will circulate giving praise and encouragement and intervening where appropriate to assist a child. She will probably articulate the responses to a task, for example, 'Tommy is stretching his arms up high when he jumps' and 'Mary is sliding backwards down the plank'. The purpose of this is threefold. In the first instance it indicates to the children that the teacher is watching and recognizing what they are doing, giving positive feedback and encouragement. Secondly, it translates the actions into words helping children with their vocabulary. Thirdly, it offers opportunity for other children to try something out. For example, Peter may not have thought of sliding backwards down the plank like Mary but having

heard Mary getting recognition will try the same action in the hope of getting similar praise for his efforts.

Children learn from the teacher. The tasks she sets may be accompanied by a demonstration of an action for them to try to copy. This can be done with virtually no verbalizing, i.e. she may say, 'come on children, follow me' and lead them around the room in a 'follow my leader' type activity in which she does a range of skipping, jumping, hopping activities. She may 'show and do' at the same time, 'can you stand on one leg like this?'

The teacher will take advantage of the fact that children also learn from each other and use demonstrations by children to illustrate a point, show good examples, identify interesting individual responses and to encourage a child who, for him, has achieved something for which the teacher feels he needs public recognition.

At the end of a lesson, perhaps whilst the children are getting changed, or sitting quietly on the carpet back in the classroom, a brief chat with the children about what they achieved, what they enjoyed and how they can get better will help to summarize the learning that has taken place, both for them and the teacher. Opportunities for the children to write about what they have done, or illustrate their achievements in some way, are often taken by class teachers during the day.

Principle 4: There should be a range of activities and sufficient time given to the subject

The National Curriculum Council identifies three areas of activity that children should experience in physical education at Key Stage 1 and if the school chooses to teach swimming to Key Stage 1 it may do so.

These are:

> Games
> Gymnastic activities
> Dance
> (Swimming)

Each of these areas has a different emphasis. It is important that during the school year a balance is maintained between games, gymnastic activities and dance.

These are not merely traditional subjects watered down from secondary school physical education, but stem from children's natural actions and activities as identified in principle 1. We are not asking children to do anything way outside their experience, and adult concepts of sport and physical education are not appropriate for this age group. Having laid the foundations in these activities, Key Stages 2, 3 and 4 can build on them as the children mature, grow stronger, learn to control their body weight and increase their knowledge and understanding.

Adult sport revolves around the element of competition and much has been written about the place of competition in the primary school. An infant is keen for recognition of his prowess, 'look at me' is his battle cry but he will not be ready for many of the skills and activities that adults are anxious for him to acquire and boredom, frustration and even injury may result.

> 'I couldn't do skipping so my heart didn't go bang, bang, bang (i.e. work hard). I spent all my time untangling the rope.'

This was the comment of a 6-year-old during an activity based on improving fitness levels in school.

A 7-year-old boy playing an eleven-a-side football game ran up and down the field calling out, 'give us a go, give us a go' to no avail. He did not touch the ball once during a thirty-minute lesson.

Rather than seeing each activity as a separate identity there will be overlap, especially in the nursery and reception classes. In the nursery a child may switch rapidly from using a stage block first to jump off and then as a car, sitting on it and saying, 'broom, broom, broom' as he turns an imaginary steering wheel and changes gear with his feet. He may then get off and impulsively run fast around the playground before using the block to jump from again.

In the reception class a child may use a skipping rope placed on the ground as a tightrope, he may then pick it up and it becomes a horse's rein, he wiggles it and it is a snake, he may also use it to skip with.

Gradually we help the children to progress from:

> being unaware of his movements (pre-school, nursery and reception) to:
> > becoming aware of his movements (Key Stage 1);
> > becoming skilfully aware of his movements (Key Stage 2);
> > becoming skilfully unaware of his movements (Key Stages 3 and 4).

More attention will be paid to each activity in subsequent chapters. Children should not be excluded from physical education except for health reasons. Lively children who cannot sit still in the classroom should not be denied their PE for being naughty since they need a physical outlet and will probably settle down more quickly in class as a result. Children should not be taken out of PE lessons for extra reading, music lesson etc., any more than they would from other curricular activities.

Physical education lessons ought not to be cancelled because the children have not finished their 'work' or 'we are too busy today'. If the hall is in use then the possibility of going outside should be explored, or a space cleared in the classroom for a dance activity perhaps.

Children should grow up knowing that exercise is important whatever the circumstances and it needs to be built into the daily programme just as eating is. Dog owners make sure they take the dog for a walk at least once a day; we, like dogs, need exercise too.

The range of activities identified by the National Curriculum Council should be linked, where possible, to other curriculum areas. Since we are concerned with the education of the whole child then to isolate physical education would be counter-productive.

Language is a common denominator and children can experience directional words in physical education, 'Let's jump backwards' for example. Words can be used to describe dance movements such as, 'He twirled round and round like a spinning top.'

Counting and measuring in games will support mathematical concepts and tracing a route taken over the large apparatus may tie in with mapping work in geography.

In the classroom discussion on 'Why do I get hot doing PE?' could arise in topic work about 'Ourselves' or 'My Body'. Games the children have made up by themselves can be collated, printed out on a computer and made into a class book, perhaps.

However, we must not lose sight of the second principle, namely, 'Children should be as active as possible during physical education' and if understanding a mathematical concept is best grasped in a physical context then surely it should be done in the time allocated to mathematics?

Principle 5: In order to achieve a balanced programme there should be sufficient equipment and adequate facilities

Physical education equipment is one of the most expensive items a school will purchase. Small equipment such as balls can easily get lost, punctured or worn out and need regular replacing. Although the initial outlay on large apparatus is expensive, apart from regular safety checks, it should last twenty years or more.

Children need a range of equipment that they can easily handle. The equipment most used in infant schools is probably a bean bag. A child can grasp it easily, slide it along the floor and throw and catch it without its bouncing all over the place. Available on the market now is a range of new, colourful and exciting equipment such as a smaller, slightly heavier version of the bean bag originally intended for mastery of the skills of juggling, and balls which are less bouncy and easier to handle. Foam javelins are safe and fun to use and can introduce children to the dynamics of flight.

Colourful and attractive plastic play balls between nine and twelve centimetres in diameter serve many purposes. Balls which do not need to be inflated regularly are now available. They can be thrown, bounced, rolled, caught, kicked or struck easily and are not so bouncy as tennis balls. Airflow balls are difficult for infants to handle as they are so light and bounce badly.

Children should be introduced to large foam balls and light footballs. Foam balls shaped like rugby balls are fun. Quoits that can be rolled, grasped easily and used in target activities provide other experiences for the children along with hoops of different sizes. Play bats, shuttle-cocks, skipping ropes of different lengths, all give opportunities for a variety of activities and games.

If the teacher is working on a specific skill such as bouncing a large ball, it is vital in the first instance that all the children have one each. If there is not enough to go round this can create all sorts of problems.

Light cones, skittles and other markers are useful and all equipment needs to be readily accessible.

The purchase of large gymnastic apparatus, because of its initial expense, needs careful consideration.

A climbing frame will provide an opportunity for the children to strengthen their arm and shoulder muscles. Ropes also help to strengthen the arms but since they swing and are flexible they provide a different experience of climbing.

Children need large solid surfaces from which they can jump with confidence. (They should not jump down from a height greater than they are as the impact is too much for their knees at this age). Thus a variety of boxes, steps, and stools or tables with rungs are necessary.

As well as the large surfaces provided by boxes, the children need narrow planks, bars, ladders and benches which can be hooked onto other pieces of apparatus at angles providing opportunities for sliding, balancing and hanging.

All the apparatus offers opportunities for exploration, discovery and gaining confidence. Children will find holes to crawl through, places to hang upside down, somewhere to see the world from a different angle and they will meet the challenges of getting on, over, along, up and off obstacles.

Children will need mats to land on when they jump down from a piece of apparatus. These should be washable, light to carry, nonslip and thick enough to prevent grounding. They provide soft surfaces for rolling and balancing actions and when spaced out in interesting formations can challenge the children to travel along unusual pathways.

Storage is always a problem. If equipment and apparatus is not easily accessible then teachers, quite rightly, fight shy of using it. Wherever possible all equipment needs to be stored near to where it is to be used.

Adequate indoor space for activities to take place safely is of paramount importance and should not be limited by displays, chairs, or pianos. Out of doors the playground is used for PE and play times. Children may spend as much as 25 per cent of the school day in the playground and there is a move towards finding ways in which the play area can be used more profitably.

The 'Learning through Landscapes' Trust was commissioned in 1991 to look at the design and management of school grounds and their use with a view to improving the environment quality and educational use of the land.

Titman (1993) writes:

> 'At least 50 per cent of the formal or National Curriculum can be taught in school grounds. In fact 20 per cent can best be learned outside: not only PE but science, maths, technology, English, drama and even religious education. Schools throughout the country are beginning to recognize this, and there are hundreds of examples of exciting and innovative ways of developing school grounds into outdoor classrooms.'

It is recognized that not all schools can provide all the equipment and resources recommended, but unless a target of what to provide is set,

schools will not know what to aim for. Maybe they should look afresh at what is available and try to make better use of the existing resources, and at the same time have a rolling plan to increase 'consumable' stock.

Principle 6: All children are entitled to the best physical education possible

All children are special and are entitled to the best we can give them. In physical education there may be children who find academic learning difficult but are very capable physically.

A few children may have problems keeping up with the other children through some physical disability. There will be children with sensory difficulties or cognitive problems, and some will have emotional and behavioural disorders.

The children may have language problems and for some, English is their second language. They will all come from different backgrounds which may be a different country, a farm in a rural community or a home in an inner city which does not allow for playing out of doors.

Whatever the problem, we need to include all children in our PE lessons as far as possible. Children who are experiencing difficulties with their learning (and there may be up to 20 per cent of them) need more physical activity, not less. They may be overprotected at home, and lacking opportunity to move about as freely as other children. This may mean that they lack strength, good muscle tone, are overweight or underdeveloped.

All children deserve a full and balanced programme of physical education and it should not be cancelled at the slightest excuse.

It is important at this stage to encourage the children because they will not have fully realized that they have any problems. If we are not careful, we will contribute towards a lack of confidence, a sense of rejection, feeling different from other children, being labelled and believing they cannot achieve.

Various researchers (Cousineau and Luke *et al.*, 1990) have identified that the children with greater ability in physical education in primary schools receive far more attention than those with less.

> 'The teacher often praised the HA (higher ability) in front of the class, thus increasing his self confidence. Conversely the LA (lower ability) often received criticism and was reprimanded in front of his peers which would have a negative effect on his self esteem.' (Whitehall and Underwood, 1991)

This was an observation made during a case study of 8-year-olds in games lessons.

One of the main causes of school phobia and truanting is the dislike of physical education. We must be careful not to sow the seeds of negative attitudes towards what should be considered fun and enjoyable.

Most of what is done in physical education lessons is good classroom practice applied in a physical environment. However, it is difficult for a class teacher to have to cope with special needs children when many of the other children are still struggling to control their actions and thus safety becomes an added concern. She will need extra help if at all possible.

As in the classroom, the teacher should begin with what the child CAN do and build on it rather than concentrating on what he can NOT do. This will mean close liaison with the parents and good observation of the child whilst he is moving and an ability to identify his problems on the part of the teacher.

Much of what we ask infants to do is of an open-ended nature and the children can respond according to their individual ability. All the children benefit from exploring and discovering what their bodies can do and how equipment can be used, they can select what they want to do and practise it, and there is no reason why any child should be excluded from this play — like experiential learning but instead he should be encouraged to integrate as much as possible.

When teaching specific skills, special needs children will benefit from having the skills broken down into small steps. This requires sound knowledge of the skill on the part of the teacher. On the market is a range of new and exciting brightly-coloured equipment adapted for children with special needs, such as bats covered in velcro to assist in catching a ball, for example. However, where modified activities or equipment are used, it is important that this is done with integrity and that the child does not feel singled out or made to feel different.

There are occasions when a child with special needs is unable to join in and this should be recognized. However, rather than excluding him, he should be given the opportunity to share the children's fun and enjoyment and hopefully, come to accept his limitations. He should not be fobbed off with what he comes to regard as 'inferior' alternatives.

Many children will be able to show that they can achieve in some aspects better than others. They might be able to contribute to the planning of a dance, for example, but not be so good at performing it.

Meeting some of the needs the children may be experiencing

There are different ways of categorizing individual needs but these can be limiting leading to the exclusion of some needs particularly experienced by children at Key Stage 1.

In order to look at entitlement for all children, consideration can be given to the following:

(i)   Any child who has difficulty in moving, whether it be temporary, permanent, mild or severe.

(ii) Children with behavioural or emotional problems.

(iii) Children finding it difficult to understand the language that is being used.

(iv) Children from other cultural backgrounds.

(v)   Particularly gifted or talented children who feel frustrated.

(vi) Entitlement regarding gender.

Each of these will be dealt with in more detail since this is such an important issue.

Physical Education for all children who have difficulties in moving

The problem may be a limb which does not function correctly, or the child may have a motor coordination problem in which the cause could lie rooted in the brain (sometimes these children are commonly referred to as clumsy children). It might be a visual handicap that has gone undetected, for example a child may not be able to put things into perspective. In this instance he will see everything as a photograph and be unable to distinguish a ball coming towards him from the background in which it is placed.

For children in this category, an intervention programme may be helpful. This involves a small group of children being taken out of lessons and given a purpose-built programme designed to meet their needs which is supervised by a physiotherapist or a volunteer with specialist knowledge, on a weekly basis.

Physical Education for all children with behavioural or emotional problems

These problems are more likely to occur at Key Stage 1 because the children are still adjusting to school life.

Children often have difficulties in socialization and in adapting their behaviour to fit in with a group or work cooperatively with a partner. This is a complex skill often taken for granted. Caplow (1964) writes:

'In every situation in which a member or an aspirant is to be transformed into a successful incumbent, there are at least four requirements to be met.
1   A new self image
    As an individual takes a position in a group he learns to define himself in response to the expectations which the group has of a person occupying that status. The person attempts to assimilate a group identity into his own identity.
2   New involvements
    When an individual joins a new group he meets new people. He finds he must modify his performance.
3   New values
    He must visualise his proposed line of action from a generalized standpoint, anticipate the reaction of others, inhibit undesirable impulses and thus guide his conduct.
4   New accomplishments
    While a team performance is in progress, any member of that team has the power to disrupt it by inappropriate behaviour. This means an observance of professional etiquette and a whole series of complex skills which must be learned to maintain the group performance at an adequate level.'

Thus we can see that the process of learning to be part of a team takes a long time and we should not push children into cooperative or competitive activities too soon. The activities need to be constructed with great care and the children introduced gradually to being part of a team so that they can work through the stages identified by Caplow.

Games and activities can be specially designed for all children to take part in helping the children to cooperate with each other. The level of skill demanded in such games should be kept to a minimum. Chapter 3 'Games in the Early Years' gives some examples.

Physical Education for all children who have difficulty in understanding English (ESL children in particular)

In many classes there are children who have English as a second language. They can be helped by watching and copying a clear demonstration by the teacher and by being paired off with another child who can show them what to do and if bilingual, can explain in the child's first language. Games which introduce parts of the body such as '*Busy Bee*' and '*Oh Grandmama*' (see chapter 2) will help. Games which name actions can also be played, for example:

> *Hop It!*
> All the children stand in hoops except one who is 'it' and one other child. The hoops are spread out in spaces. The child without a hoop runs and stands in another child's hoop and shouts, 'hop it'. The child who is 'it' then chases the child who has had to leave his hoop but they must both hop. If he is caught he becomes 'it'. The child being chased then stands in another hoop and says, 'jump it'. The game continues as before with a different action being called out each time.

Games can be played in which the children are introduced to directions and this can also be experienced in gymnastic activities and dance.

Prepositional language can be reinforced in games, such as:

> '*Bazonka*':
> Each child stands in a hoop. On the command 'on the land' he stands outside the hoop. On the command 'in the sea' he puts his hands in the hoop, and on the command, 'in the air' he puts his hands in the air. On the word BAZONKA he runs round the room. On the command 'stop' he freezes and then finds another hoop to stand in.

In gymnastic activities the children can experience standing ON a mat, jumping OFF a box, crawling UNDER a ladder etc. The teacher must use these terms clearly over and over again until the children can link the words with what they are doing.

Physical Education for all children from other cultural backgrounds

One of the strengths of teaching early years' children is the close liaison with the parents. Class teachers have the opportunity to discuss what they are hoping to achieve in physical education and to outline the school's policy when they meet the parents. Since all children are collected from school by an adult, the teacher can discover their attitudes to physical activity.

Parents may find physical education strange. Some do not pay particular attention to the value of play and may need help in understanding the importance of physical play which forms the basis of physical education.

There may be concerns regarding getting changed for PE, going barefoot, swimming in mixed groups, wearing PE clothing, keeping the legs covered and coping with turbans. These problems can be ironed out by talking to the parents and winning their support.

The richness of diversity can be considered as a resource and the children can share games and dances which form part of their heritage. This can be done in lessons, or at an assembly. A class book of games from other countries could be made by the children perhaps with the help of parents describing the games they used to play. Parents, too, may be able to teach some simple dance steps to the children.

This will help fulfil one of the programmes of study at Key Stage 1 in the dance activities, namely:

> 'Pupils should be taught to perform movements or patterns, including some from existing dance traditions.' (National Curriculum Physical Education)

Physical Education for all children who are exceptionally gifted or have particular talents in this field

Some children come to school having outstanding potential which may be innate, hereditary or acquired through parental encouragement, and teachers may feel apprehensive about how to handle this, particularly if the children appear very daring, overconfident, without fear or are unaware of others. There is a danger that some children may try to emulate them causing accidents.

Teachers should try to structure the tasks to allow for all levels of ability, although young children are often quite happy to consolidate what they already can do. Handled with sensitivity, confidence can be developed without making other children jealous. Care should be taken not to use a child to demonstrate a movement if that movement is way beyond the capabilities of the rest. Even the more talented can be challenged to be more inventive, more versatile or more exact in the performance.

The teacher's role, as has been stated already, is to build on what the child can do, not to introduce completely new concepts out of the range of the child's understanding and ability. Exceptional children can be extended by introducing them to extra-curricular activities or clubs after school. But it should be remembered that if they are pushed too far there is a danger of permanent injury to the body, they may lose interest quickly, and their understanding of what they are doing is sacrificed to the value placed on performance.

Physical Education for all children regardless whether they are girls or boys

Children should be given equal opportunity to develop their potential to the full. There is no reason why girls should not take part in all physical activities on equal terms with the boys. Care should be taken to see that all children get the same amount of attention in lessons and are not 'crowded out' by the over-exuberant ones. This is most likely to happen when the children start school, because some are very timid whilst others are full of confidence.

If the school has a policy of nonsegregation then girls and boys will partner each other in paired activities and will line up at the door together. There should be no suggestion that dance is a 'girly' activity and football only for the boys.

Groups working together should be mixed and both girls and boys should learn to carry the large apparatus in gymnastic activities. All children can help to set out and put away the games equipment.

Where to go for help and support within the community

It is worthwhile trying to enlist extra help where possible at no additional cost, although it is appreciated that sensitivity and sympathy are vital requirements of anyone prepared to assist. Teachers need to work closely with helpers so that they know exactly what is expected of them.

The National Curriculum Physical Education non-statutory Guidance, (NCC, 1992) state:

> 'Physical education teachers should seek partnerships with:
> parents;
> special needs coordinators;
> support specialists, for example, physiotherapists;
> support staff;
> outside agencies, for example, the British Sports Association for the Disabled.'

Added to this list could be the help of older pupils, such as secondary school students during their general studies or after examinations, adults who are enthusiastic sports players such as local coaches at leisure centres, or retired grandparents who have expertise in bringing up children.

To summarize therefore:

(i)   All children are entitled to a balanced physical education programme and no child discriminated against. (This includes children being excluded because they have forgotten their kit, have not finished their classroom work, are taken out of PE to attend other activities or lessons such as learning support sessions or have been naughty.)

(ii) Programmes can be modified or adapted by differentiation of task or outcome.

(iii) Equipment can be adapted to meet individual needs.

(iv) Skills can be broken down and taught step by step.

(v) The teacher should start with what the child can do and build on it (principle 1).

(vi) PE must be fun, constructive and safe and promote self esteem and confidence.

(vii) Help can be obtained from a variety of sources within the community.

(viii) At first children may depend totally on adult support and then gradually the dependency becomes shared between the adult and the child. The aim is for the child to become independent of adult help whilst moving.

The planning process with these principles in mind

These six basic principles form the foundation on which a physical education programme at Key Stage 1 can be built. Chapters 2 to 6 give details of the curriculum content and areas of experience the children should have. The material can be used to plan the curriculum according to the needs of the children in each particular school and it is not anticipated that all the ideas will be appropriate for everyone, so careful selection is necessary. Nor is it intended that this book should become a practical resource that can be picked up at the 'eleventh hour'. It endeavours to put physical education into perspective giving meaning and understanding to the subject as well as providing theoretical and practical ideas for both students and class teachers.

Each of the chapters 3, 4, 5 and 6 gives guidance on the planning at three levels, namely:

overall planning — how to compile a statement based on identifying the needs of the children and ways to meet these needs;

year planning — establishing units of work each lasting six weeks;

lesson plans — detailed planning by the class teacher.

This is followed by criteria for evaluation of the success of the programme. Planning is, in the main, related to each age group although it is recognized that children progress at different rates and are often taught in mixed age groups. Teachers are used to dealing with this situation and need to draw on their expertise to decide how to adapt ideas to suit their children.

Lesson plans will follow a set procedure, namely:

warming up activities — these are designed to get the children physically prepared, used to the space and aware of the need to listen carefully to instructions;

development of the unit of work — the main input by the teacher takes place in this section of the lesson and new ideas are introduced and practised;

using these ideas — in games lessons this may be the playing of a game or a skills circuit, in gymnastic activities it will be the work on the large apparatus and in dance it may be making up a class dance;

calming down activities — these are designed to lower the level of excitement, help the children to relax and walk quietly back to the classroom.

A bank of ideas for warming up activities and calming down activities which can be used for games, gymnastic activities and dance lessons can be found at the end of this chapter.

Overall planning as a whole school policy is dealt with in greater detail in chapter 7.

The teaching process with these principles in mind

There is a close relationship between the teaching strategies in the classroom and during physical education lessons. Teachers do not always recognize this. Giving simple instructions to the whole class at the start of a session by sitting the children down (on the carpet in the classroom) setting tasks and getting an overview of how the children are responding, working the children in groups, circulating, encouraging and helping and finally drawing the children together for feedback and evaluation of the activity, is normal procedure both in the classroom and in the hall or out of doors.

Generally the overall process can be summarized as follows:

> set the task — give verbal instructions and visual demonstration;
> watch the class working — get overview of the response and give encouragement;
> observe individuals — give 'public' feedback, i.e. 'I can see Peter is pointing his toes nicely';
> choose a child to demonstrate a teaching point;
> discuss with the children what they have just seen;
> help individual children by making suggestions;
> improve quality of performance — for example, 'stretch your fingers when you balance';
> look at good performances — discuss with the children why they are good;
> give time for the children to practise;
> set the next task.

The place of demonstration

It is recognized that children learn from doing, from the teacher and from each other, therefore in a practical subject such as physical education, it is important that the children are given visual pictures of what to do as well as verbal instructions, although these may be suggestions rather than specific movement patterns for them to follow.

Demonstration by the teacher

> 'The visual image . . . can have considerable impact on the observers' subsequent attempts to improve their performance. Teachers frequently make use of demonstrations as a means of providing a clearer picture of what is to be attempted.' (Cross, 1991)

Visual pictures are particularly important for children from different ethnic backgrounds. For some, physical activity may be a somewhat strange phenomenon. This is even more bewildering if English is a second language.

This means, of course, that the teacher must be suitably attired in order to demonstrate. The minimum requirement being safe footwear.

The teacher may say to the children, 'Jump up and down like this' and show them what to do. If the task is more open-ended she may say, 'Find a way of jumping like this, or find another way.' Thus she is giving two examples for those who need them but leaving an alternative for the more inventive.

There will be times when the teacher needs to show the children how to start an action. In this instance she may say, 'Put your hands on the floor and then stretch one foot up in the air.' As she speaks she will place her hands on the floor but leave the children to find their own way of stretching one foot.

Similarly, she may need to show the children how to end a movement without doing the whole sequence, for example, 'At the end of a forward roll you should stretch out your arms like this.'

On the apparatus she can extend the range of movements by making suggestions such as, 'Try putting your hands further up the rope when you swing' showing the child where to put his hands at the same time.

In games she may show the children how to bounce a ball or say, 'Stand facing your partner like this' and then, having shown them where to position themselves say, 'Now bounce the ball to your partner' without actually doing so herself.

Demonstrations by the children

The teacher may select a child to demonstrate an action because it is just possible he is better at it than she is. She might say, 'Watch how Peter does a forward roll.' This would be followed by a discussion on what Peter did, how he tucked his head in and where he put his hands and then she could say, 'Now you try to roll like Peter did' (checking that all the children know the safety factors).

Children may be chosen to demonstrate because they have responded to a task by performing with good quality. For example, the teacher may say, 'Look at how Peter rolls the ball'. If the response is particularly original she might say, 'Peter has found a good way to roll the ball, try to do the same.'

Sometimes a teacher may choose a child to show the others what he has done because, for him, this has been a great achievement and all the class can share in his success.

The teacher should ascertain with the child first that he is prepared to demonstrate and he must be clear what it is he is going to show, or he may change it at the last minute.

All demonstrations need to be a learning situation and should be followed up by a brief discussion with the children. They should not be used to show poor quality work or as an example of what not to do.

Occasionally children can work in pairs, one performing and the other observing with a view to helping the performer to improve. This must be a positive experience for both children and used only with sensitivity.

The teacher should not always choose those who go to gymnastics' clubs, especially if the

model demonstration is unattainable by most of the children watching.

Half the class watching the other half is non-productive. It is impossible to watch so many at once and the children tend to 'switch off'. The time is better spent with the children being active.

Definitions of some of the terms used in physical education

This is an attempt to clarify and simplify the technical terminology in order to help students and teachers when trying to put the basic principles into practice.

Ability

Natural talent to perform effectively, determined by genetics and experience and requires intrinsic motivation.

Action

The way the body moves and the manner in which it operates. Actions are innate and usually fully developed by the age of 7. Actions are the simplest of movements and require a certain degree of force, coordination and integration of different parts of the body, each action needs to be carried out at a certain speed in order to be effective.

Activity

The involvement in a pursuit which has a specific purpose. Physical activities usually require quick, lively movements, often repetitious.

Aesthetic awareness

Intrinsic knowing that a movement or movement pattern is performed in a way that is pleasing to watch and conforms to the observer's criteria of appreciation of something beautiful.

Assessment

Means by which pupils' attainment is observed and recorded using agreed criteria understood by both pupils and teachers and based on End of Key Stage Descriptions. In physical education it should be continuous and on going. Pupils' efforts as well as ability should be taken into consideration.

Body awareness

A means of helping a performer to feel what is going on in his body by making him responsible for his own actions and paying attention to each part of the body involved in that action.

Competition

A significant driving force within an individual which directly or indirectly influences his status within the environment. It cannot be ignored or totally repressed but needs to be effectively channelled in order to enhance self esteem.

'The competitive spirit is deeply ingrained in the nature of man. It is an expression of man's biological inheritance, for man in his own evolution has been forced to compete for survival in an environment which has often been hostile and dangerous.' (Rarick, 1973)

Cooperation

A process involving interaction between one person and others in which the individual has to learn to adapt and modify skills and behaviour in order to accomplish a specific task which could not be achieved individually.

Demonstration

A visual model for a performer attempting a skill so that he has a picture of what it should look like.

Evaluation

Evaluation is a process designed to give meaningful feedback. In physical education it is used to help improve performance and requires careful observation and an ability to diagnose and rectify errors. It determines whether established targets have been met, to record progress and give insight to individual childrens' potential. Evaluation should also be used to determine if teaching methods are appropriate.

Exercise

Regular and/or repeated use of the body in order to strengthen muscles, increase stamina and endurance, improve the flexibility of the joints and increase the heart rate.

Feedback

Information received by the learner after performance designed to improve that performance.

Learning

A change in an individual involving the process of assimilation of new skills, experiences, knowledge and understanding affecting attitude and behaviour.

Locomotor development

Progressive stages of a child leading to upright movement in which the body can travel from one place to another involving rolling, pivoting, rocking, sliding, crawling, climbing, running, jumping and throwing.

Manual dexterity

The use of hands and arms to carry out fine motor skills.

Maturation skills

These require coordination, balance and other behavioural patterns and develop in the same sequence in all children.

Movement pattern

The way in which the body as a whole unit moves in relation to its environment. Movement patterns are a series of linked movements involved in changes to the body both in position, place and posture.

Motor skills

Movements of any part of the body which are the result of neuromuscular action. Fine motor skills require small muscle groups and are used in developing speaking, reading, writing etc. Gross motor skills use large muscle groups as in walking, running and jumping.

Physical Education

Physical Education is a structured programme of educational experiences in which physical activity is of paramount importance.

Recreation

Physical activity in which the performer participates through choice.

Skill

The word skill has many uses. In physical skill we are referring to a learned activity which has a recognised outcome and is performed efficiently and economically. It is the end result of a chain of nervous system activity.

Sport

Specific competitive activities including games and athletics in which winning is the main objective.

Technique

'Precise movement patterns which, if executed at the right time and in the right manner reveal fluent skilled performance.' (*ibid*)

Warming up activities — a bank of tasks that can be used at the start of lessons

1   Run anywhere, stop when I clap my hands
2   Skip anywhere, stop when I clap my hands
3   Jump anywhere, stop when I bang the tambourine
4   Walk anywhere, stop when I put my hands in the air
5   Hop anywhere, stop when I shake the tambourine
6   Run, when I call out a colour touch something of that colour and stand still
7   Run around, lifting your knees high in the air
8   Run around, taking large steps
9   Run around, taking small steps
10 Run around, taking large strides
11 Run around, crossing your feet as you go
12 Walk backwards, look over your shoulder to see where you are going
13 Pretend you have paint on your feet. Spread the paint all over the playground by running everywhere

14 Run, stop when I clap my hands and stretch up high

15 Run, stop when I bang the drum and tuck up small

16 Run, when I say 'Change' find a different way of going along

17 Start to run slowly, gradually get faster

18 Run fast, gradually get slower

19 Skip anywhere, when I bang the drum stop and make a wide shape with your body

20 Hop anywhere, when I clap my hands stop and make a tall shape

21 Run around, try to overtake three other children

22 Run in and out of each other

23 Walk around as low as you can then walk as high as you can

24 Run around, when I call out, 'One' stop and make a tall shape, when I call out, 'Two' stop and make a wide shape, when I call out, 'Three' tuck up small

25 'Follow My Leader' — teacher as leader

26 'Follow My Leader' — child as leader, lines of five or six children

27 Jump up and down on your magic spot

28 Jog on your magic spot getting your knees high

29 Jog on your magic spot getting quicker and quicker

30 On your magic spot, copy the teacher who will jog, jump, run etc.

31 Hop along a line, run along another line, skip along another line.

32 Do star jumps on your magic spot

33 Find a magic spot, run away, return when I blow the whistle

34 Jump up and down on your magic spot

35 Find anywhere you have not been to before and hop on the spot

36 Jump forwards, backwards and sideways

37 Play the 'Space Game'. Run anywhere. 'Freeze' in a space when I say, 'Stop'. If all the children are in spaces they score a point. If they are not spread out in spaces the teacher scores a point. Do this three times to see who is the winner

38 Play the 'Mars Bar Game.' Pretend there are Mars bars on the ground and Milky Ways hanging from the trees. Run anywhere, when I call out, 'Mars bars' pretend to pick up a Mars bar by touching the ground. When I call out, 'Milky Ways' jump up in the air as if picking a Milky Way off a tree.

Calming down activities — a bank of tasks that can be used at the end of lessons

1 Walk slowly in and out of each other

2 Jog quietly round the room

3 Do little bouncy jumps on your magic spot

4 Do big jumps on your magic spot, gradually make the jumps smaller

5 Hop on your magic spot

6 Walk backwards slowly, look over your shoulder to see where you are going

7 Stand on your magic spot, stretch up tall with your hands high in the air

8 Stand on your magic spot, stretch out as wide as you can

9 Do ten star jumps then stand quietly

10 Run on your magic spot getting your knees high, gradually slow down

11 Stand still, circle your arms round and round slowly

12 Walk in and out of each other. 'Freeze' when you hear the tambourine

13 Tuck up small on the floor. Gradually grow up until you are standing as I shake the tambourine

14 Tuck up small on the floor. Line up quietly when someone touches you

15 Tuck up small on the floor. Stretch out one arm and then the other. Slowly stand up

16 Creep round the room on tip toes. Line up when you hear your name

17 Tuck up small on your magic spot. When you hear me call out a colour, line up if you are wearing something of that colour

18 Practise something you have done in the lesson. 'Freeze' when I call your name

19 Practise something you have done in the

lesson. Line up quietly when I call out the first letter of your name

20 Tuck up small on your magic spot. The teacher will say the poem:

> Hidden in the beehive, where are the bees?
> Hidden away where nobody sees,
> But soon they come creeping out of the hive,
> One, two, three, four, five.

Line up quietly as the teacher says the last line

21 All say the poem:

> This old elephant does not like to race
> He prefers to plod at a gentle pace
> One, two, three, four, five.

As the poem is being recited the children walk slowly round the room and line up on the last line

22 Sit on the floor and copy the teacher's hand gestures.

Chapter Two

Laying the Foundations in the Nursery

Introduction

Why include movement education in the nursery?

The movement experiences the child gains before he starts school will depend on many factors. Much of his activity will be self-motivated and he will be 'on the go' most of his waking hours. It is hoped that his parents will have played with him, bouncing him up and down on their knees, swinging him round and round, chasing him, and engaging in a range of 'rough and tumble' type romps. He will have visited recreation grounds and enjoyed the sensation of sliding and swinging together with a chance to climb up ladders and crawl through tunnels. He will have gone walking and possibly been taken swimming.

He may have older brothers and sisters who have included him in their games, maybe with a ball, or activities of a 'make believe' nature such as 'Cowboys and Indians' and although he might not know much about what is going on he is applying his locomotor skills, developing his concepts and learning to socialize.

'. . . since the large movements of the body ripen first, the gross-motor activity precedes competency in respect of fine motor and language development. It may, therefore, be suggested that physical play is not only a prerequisite for physical and emotional development, but it is also the most accessible and natural vehicle to use in the promotion of the development of the children's intellect.' (Tanner, 1978)

So we can see how important movement is as a medium for learning. At the same time we need to make sure that our children are receiving a structured programme allowing for development and progression to take place.

Botham, Early Years Inspector for Cumbria writes:

'Nursery education should be planned and should have aims and objectives. It should be assessed just as it is when the children are in the reception class. We are very strong on the emphasis that it is about education but from a play base.' (Botham in Adams, 1993)

What then are the physical needs of children in the nursery?

(i)   To extend their physical world, meeting new situations such as sloping surfaces to slide down, climbing frames to go up, holes to crawl through, rails to turn upside down on, moving objectives to climb on such as swings and see-saws.

(ii)   To be able to run, jump, roll, spin, hop, in safety.

(iii)   To develop spatial awareness by using mobile toys such as tricycles and wheelbarrows.

(iv)   To develop body awareness, for example, the feet can be used to stamp, take big steps, walk on tip toes.

(v)   Be introduced to the handling of moving objects such as balls, bean bags, quoits, hoops, tyres and balloons.

(vi)   To discover how to move through water

and learn first hand about buoyancy, flotation, making waves and splashing.

(vii) To have opportunities for imaginative play, role play, stories in movement, expressive movement, and rhythmic movements.

(viii) To develop concepts such as up and down, over, under, high and low through movement.

(ix) To learn how to share, take turns, be aware of and play along side and with other children.

How can we meet these needs?

By providing:

(i) a structured framework in which children can explore a range of possibilities and build up movement patterns, gain confidence and develop at their own pace, such as climbing frames, slides, poles and tunnels;

(ii) a grass area with banks and slopes for rough and tumble games;

(iii) a safe, hard area for the children to ride their bicycles, tricycles, trucks and push prams, trolleys, and wheelbarrows;

(iv) an indoor space for:
    (a) play with balls, bean bags, hoops and skipping ropes;
    (b) guided activities giving opportunities for expressive and rhythmic movement;
    (c) directed activities based on body awareness, spatial awareness and relationships;
    (d) opportunity for children to move through water in paddling pools or learner pools.

What is the role of the teacher in developing movement education in the nursery?

'The ladder of education can never be secure unless the first rung is firmly in place.' (Peacock, 1994)

The teacher should not dominate the activities of children but should take a positive role in their physical development. This is done by:

(i) Safety considerations
    (a) The safety of the children must come first.
    (b) Suitable clothing should be worn by the children. If they are climbing they should not wear anything that is liable to catch such as an unfastened anorak. Slippery shoes cause the most accidents. If indoors bare feet are safest providing the floor is suitable.
    (c) Simple ground rules such as no touching, pushing, and only one child on a piece of apparatus at a time where appropriate, should be established and maintained at all times.
    (d) National and County regulations concerning safety surfaces, height and construction of apparatus must be strictly adhered to.
    (e) Close supervision is necessary.

(ii) Careful observation of:
    (a) children's physical behaviour in a variety of situations;
    (b) social interaction between peers;
    (c) development in other aspects such as language and imagination;
    (d) keeping records of the progress of the children. Their coordination, skill, competence and confidence should be noted, as well as how they relate to other children in different situations. If children are identified as having any particular problems then efforts should be made to help them overcome the difficulties without undermining what confidence they may have.

(iii) Providing opportunities for children to explore, discover, and gain confidence, the children should be encouraged to become independent and self-directed.

(iv) Intervening where appropriate giving

support and encouragement, extending and challenging them, and building on their established movement patterns.

(v) Directing children's activities by the teaching of specific skills such as catching a large ball, doing 'bunny hops' skipping and playing simple traditional games such as 'Farmer's in his den'.

(vi) Be aware of the hierarchical structure of movement forms and have a knowledge of children's physical development and behaviour.

> 'We want to make sure that moving up into the reception class is smooth, so we aim to provide consistency and progression. We structure learning activities so that children are always involved in first-hand experience or practical tasks to enable them to become independent. We aim to offer experiences relevant to their future learning, and a range of activities to develop each individual child.' (Casey in Adams, 1993)

Curriculum content — areas of experience the children should have in the nursery

How can we categorize movement education to ensure a 'balanced' programme?

The National Curriculum Physical Education document divides Key Stage 1 into four areas of activity, namely games, gymnastic activities, dance and swimming (optional). However, these headings are not really appropriate in the nursery as they are too specific. To simplify the classification we can look at where the activities take place, namely, indoors, outdoors or in a pool. These can be sub-divided depending on whether or not equipment is to be used.

Not all nurseries will have the good fortune to be ideally provided with the recommended spaces and equipment, but those responsible for the curriculum will have the ability to make the best use of what is available.

Throughout all physical education we are looking at the movement of the body as the prime consideration. Small children do not make this distinction. Whilst playing they are using all their mental and physical resources at once. For the purposes of trying to focus on movement education, anything which is of secondary importance, such as drama, role play, and using construction toys is not included in this categorization. This is not to deny their importance, merely to try to simplify what is, in fact, a very complex structure.

So we are looking in detail at the following:

(i) Indoor activities without the use of equipment or apparatus
Such as:

(a) basic actions performed on the spot and moving about, and familiarization of different parts of the body and what they can do;

(b) ways to introduce children to an awareness of the space around them and how it can be used;

(c) teaching specific physical skills that children ought to master by the age of 4+;

(d) doing stories in movement — the teacher acting as narrator, and the children doing appropriate actions all together which they have either agreed on before hand or choose individually to do as the story is told;

(e) moving to music — using different kinds of music and sounds for the children to respond spontaneously, such as fast, lively music, slow, dreamy music, words, and songs.

(ii) Indoor activities using equipment and apparatus
Such as:

(a) climbing, scrambling, sliding, rocking, and jumping over, on and off large apparatus;

(b)   being introduced to small moving objects — balls, bean bags, quoits, hoops, and balloons.

(iii)   Outdoor activities using equipment and apparatus
Such as:

(a)   playing with large mobile toys — tricycles, prams, trolleys, wheelbarrows;

(b)   climbing on frames, trestles and see-saws.

(iv)   Indoor or outdoor activities
Such as class games:

(a)   traditional games involving everybody;

(b)   made up games;

(c)   parachute games;

(d)   games play with unusual equipment — giant balls, space hoppers and car tyres.

(v)   Moving through water
This activity will be described in more detail in chapter 6.

It is not appropriate in the nursery to provide sample lesson plans as found in chapters 3, 4, 5 and 6 because the activities are not structured in the same way. The time is more flexible and the sessions can either be informal, with equipment being provided for the children to play with, or more formal in which case the teacher will pose challenges using the key questions outlined below.

These are suggestions for each category, under the appropriate headings, for teachers to use as a guide, giving ideas of activities to do with the children.

1   INDOOR ACTIVITIES WITHOUT THE USE OF EQUIPMENT OR APPARATUS

(a)   **Basic actions performed on the spot and moving about, and familiarization of different parts of the body and what they can do.**

All the following ideas can be introduced by asking questions such as:

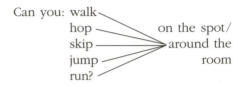

Can you: walk
hop   on the spot/
skip   around the
jump   room
run?

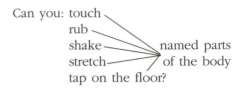

Can you: touch
rub
shake   named parts
stretch   of the body
tap on the floor?

Can you: copy me
follow me
do this
shall we play?

For example can you:
stretch up in the air like me?
follow me as I run round the room?
can you jump up and down on the spot?
shall we play 'Farmer's in his den?'

Ideas for using the feet
Walking, running, skipping, galloping, stamping, creeping, shaking, stretching in the air, tapping on the floor.
Big steps, little steps, on tip toes, heels, insteps, outsides of feet.
Go forwards, backwards, sideways.
Stand on one leg.

Ideas for using the fingers (sitting down)
Shake, stretch, hide, clap.
'Play the piano'.
Punch, make fists, make fingers.
Drum on the floor.
Play finger games — Incy Wincy Spider etc.

Ideas for using the hands and the feet
Crawling, bunny hops, making bridges.

Ideas for using the knees
Kneeling down
Walking on feet and holding knees, walk with no knees (straight legs).
Skip and get knees high, jump and get knees high.
Sit and stretch legs out in front, bend knees.
Lie and stretch knees high in the air.

Ideas for using the elbows
Wave, circle, touch, rub.
Tap on the floor (kneeling).
Tap knees and elbows together.

Ideas for using tummies and bottoms
Slide on them, balance on them, shuffle on them.
Rock on them, spin on them, wriggle on them.

Ideas for using the head
Shake, nod, roll around.

Action songs with emphasis on parts of the body
For example:
'Here we go round the Mulberry Bush'
'Head, shoulders, knees and toes'
'If you're happy and you know it'
'I wiggle my fingers'
'Two little hands go clap, clap, clap'
'Five little monkeys jumping on the bed'

(b) Ways to introduce children to an awareness of the space around them and how it can be used

(i) *The space in the room*
Pretend you have paint on your feet. Run everywhere and paint the floor.

Play 'Follow My Leader' — the teacher will lead the children all around the room.

Run in and out of everybody without touching anyone.

Give the children 'magic spots' — marks on the floor, carpet tiles, a home or a base. Children run anywhere and on a signal from the teacher they return to their 'home' or 'magic spot'.

Run around the room with your arms out like an aeroplane.

Other activities other than running can be used, for example, hopping, walking, skipping.

(ii) *The space around the body*
Pretend you are in a bubble, stroke the insides of your bubble with your hands.

Stretch up high, filling your bubble. Curl up small as if in a tiny bubble.

Walk around inside your bubble taking big/small steps.

Sit down in a big bubble. Reach out to the edges of your bubble.

Sit and spin round inside your bubble.

Walk around inside your bubble on your hands and feet.

Pretend you are a giant and take big steps around the room, stretching out your arms as well.

Pretend you are 'Tom Thumb' and go around the room making yourself as small as you can.

Play 'Jack in a Box'.

(c) Teaching specific skills that children ought to master by the age of 4+

(i) *Walking*
Head up high, in a straight line, swinging the arms, stopping safely, changing direction, ability to swerve, dodge and avoid other children.

Walk 'like a soldier', march and count, march saying 'left, right' march and 'freeze' when you hear a tambourine being shaken.

(ii) *Running*

Bend the arms, lift the knees, look where you are going, stop safely, ability to swerve, dodge and avoid other children.

Run anywhere, 'freeze' when you hear the tambourine being shaken and then banged.

Jog around the room, putting your feet on the floor quietly and carefully.

(iii) *Jumping*

On the spot — bend the knees on take-off and on landing.

Do bouncy jumps around the room.

Play 'Five Little Monkeys Jumping on the Bed'

(iv) *Hopping*

Hopping on the spot. Going along.

Keep the action brief — a strain on the supporting leg.

(v) *Balance*

Keeping as still as a statue on hands and feet, knees and elbows, tummies, bottoms, backs.

(vi) *Bending and twisting*

Explore which parts of the body will bend.

Stand up, bend over and touch your toes.

Sit down, bend and touch your toes out in front of you.

Stand up and bend your arms in lots of different ways.

Twist round to look behind you — what can you see?

(d) Stories in movement — teacher as narrator, children do appropriate actions all together, or choose individually as the story is being told

Points:

(i) There is no need to do the whole story in movement, just pick out parts which lend themselves to doing with actions.

(ii) Tell the whole story but pause when the children are to do the actions.

(iii) Choose a story that the children are very familiar with.

(iv) Be careful to use the right words or the children will correct you!

(v) Practise the movements first, for example, say to the children 'Show me how Jack climbs up on the beanstalk. Take big steps and remember to use your arms.' Or 'how do you think Jack climbed up the beanstalk? Show me.'

(vi) Do not allocate parts to individual children, they will be quite happy being all the characters themselves.

(vii) If you cannot think of an action to go with part of the story, then ask the children for ideas. Watch what they do and choose a good one for them all to do.

Examples:

The whole story is not reproduced here. The parts of the story that the children can do actions to are identified.

The Three Little Pigs

1   Once upon a time there were three little pigs who set out to find homes for themselves.
    All trot around the room.

2   The first little pig built himself a house made of straw.
    All build houses by using big, strong, heavy lifting actions.

3   A wolf came along and knocked on the door.
    All walk along like a wolf taking big steps.

4   The wolf huffed and he puffed and he blew the house down.
    All fall over.

5   The second little pig built himself a house made of sticks.
    All build houses.

6   The wolf came along and knocked on the door.
All walk along like a wolf.

7   The wolf huffed and he puffed and he blew the house down.
All fall over.

8   The third little pig built himself a house made of bricks.
All build houses.

9   The wolf came along and knocked on the door.
All walk along like a wolf.

10   The wolf tumbled down the chimney and fell into a big pot of soup with a splash.
All climb up by doing big actions lifting knees high and then fall over.

The Turnip

1   One morning in the spring a man planted some turnip seeds.
All do digging actions and stamping the ground.

2   One turnip began to grow faster than all the rest.
All curl up and then grow very big.

3   So he tried to pull the big turnip out of the ground.
All do pulling actions.

4   His wife came to help. She pulled the man and the man pulled the turnip.
One child pulls another who stands in front of him.

5   His son came to help. The boy pulled his mother, his mother pulled his father and his father pulled the turnip.
Three children pull. One behind the other.

6   Repeat for dog, hen, cock.

7   Whoosh! Up came the turnip out of the ground, and they all fell over in a heap.
All pull in a line and fall over, carefully.

The Three Billy Goats Gruff

1   Littlest Billy Goat Gruff went safely across the bridge.
All walk carefully on tip toes.

2   The next brother, Big Billy Goat Gruff, went across the bridge and up the hill to join his brother.
All walk taking big steps.

3   At once the troll jumped out from underneath the bridge and reached up to catch him.
All jump up and down like trolls.

4   But big Billy Goat Gruff was very strong and he butted the troll hard with his great horns. He tossed him high in the air and then . . . splash! Down . . . down . . . down . . . he went and fell into the middle of the river.
All fall over.

5   Big Billy Goat Gruff laughed as he ran across the bridge and up the hillside to join his two brothers.
All run up the hillside.

Little Red Riding Hood

1   Little Red Riding Hood went for a walk through the woods to see her grandmother.
All skip in and out of the trees.

2   As she was walking along the path she met a wolf.
All walk like a wolf taking big steps.

3   The wolf climbed into grandma's bed and tried to hide himself.
All curl up on the floor.

4   And he jumped out of bed and ate up Little Red Riding Hood.
All jump up and do eating movements.

5   The woodchopper chopped off the wolf's head.
All do large chopping actions.

6   Little Red Riding Hood thanked the woodcutter and ran home to her mother.
All run fast all around the room.

2 INDOOR ACTIVITIES USING EQUIPMENT AND APPARATUS

(a) Large apparatus

A range of apparatus should be provided for the children to explore, giving them experience of movement on another level other than ground level.

Climbing frames

There is a skill in climbing which involves balance, coordination and an awareness of where to place the hands and feet. Climbing requires a certain amount of confidence and daring and gives the child an opportunity to see the 'world' from another angle.

Bars can be fastened across climbing frames giving opportunities for hanging and swinging, thus strengthening children's arm and shoulder muscles.

Slides

Sliding is a pleasurable action which demands a certain amount of daring. Children enjoy the sensation of moving fast with a minimum amount of effort and at the same time are experiencing friction. They have the choice of which part of their bodies they use to slide on and have to make decisions about how and when to stop.

Boxes, tables and stools

Low boxes with large surfaces provide the children with objects to stand on and jump off. Mats should be placed where children are likely to jump from a height, and no child should jump from anything higher than themselves. They should be taught to land correctly, i.e. on both feet with knees bent.

Planks

These can be hooked on to tables with bars or struts on them, providing bridges for them to cross, hang underneath, to jump from or slide down.

All apparatus should be purpose made and there must be no improvisation. Barrels, tubes, tunnels etc. also provide opportunity for exploration and the element of adventure in experiencing something a little 'scary' by going through an enclosed space. Tunnels do not provide handles to hold on to offering a different challenge from the climbing frame.

Apparatus provides opportunity to develop prepositional language such as 'on', 'over', 'through'. It develops predicting, estimating, and decision making skills.

Children are aware of the different 'feel' to pieces of apparatus and learn the names, colours and shapes of the different pieces.

(b) Introduction to small moving objects

A selection of different sized soft balls, including rugby ball foam shapes should be made available for the children from time to time. They should not be played with where large apparatus is set out.

Teachers can throw large balls gently to individual children and teach them how to catch.

Children can be encouraged to kick, roll, and throw balls into spaces and chase after them.

Children need to experience the rolling of quoits and hoops and have the opportunity to play with balloons occasionally.

3 OUTDOOR ACTIVITIES USING EQUIPMENT AND APPARATUS

(a) Playing with mobile toys

Children should have a selection of ride-on toys and push-along toys. They will be developing specific gross motor skills and coordination such as that needed to pedal a tricycle. They will be developing their spatial awareness as they steer themselves around the playground.

They will be experiencing travelling in different directions and be building up a concept of different forces as they try to start the tricycle moving and try to stop it again.

They will be learning the limits of safety to protect themselves and others.

They will be engaging in aerobic activity thus maintaining and developing physical fitness and strengthening their legs.

There may be opportunities to introduce simple road safety activities. Pedestrian crossings can be marked out in the playground and the children can be taught both to stop at the crossing if on a tricycle and the correct procedure for crossing as a pedestrian.

(b) Climbing frames, swings and see-saws
These are often permanent fixtures out of doors and need to comply with safety regulations.

Children learn how to use their bodies to increase momentum on a swing and/or seesaw. They learn about balance and experience the sensations of going backwards and forwards and up and down through the air by their own efforts and using gravitational forces.

4 INDOOR AND OUTDOOR ACTIVITIES — Class Games

(a) Traditional games
Traditional games played by a group of children is part of our national heritage. Children become aware of belonging to a group as well as being

introduced to the concepts of rules that govern the game.

These games include 'Grandmother's Footsteps', 'What's the Time Mr Wolf', 'Simon Says', 'Follow-my-Leader' etc. Children should not be eliminated and the emphasis should be put on the taking part rather than winning or losing.

(b) Made-up games
Teachers should be able to make up simple games for the children to suit their needs, and to create situations for the children to make up their own games by providing a range of equipment and letting them play spontaneously. Here are two examples:

Oh Grandmama
The children walk about and when the teacher says, 'Oh Grandmama what a big HEAD you've got' the children have to walk anywhere holding their heads. She then repeats the words but chooses a different part of the body each time.

When she calls out, 'The wolf is coming' the children have to curl up on the spot and hide as much of their bodies as they can.

Sausages
The children stand in a space. The teacher calls out a part of the body and they have to touch that part, i.e. if she says, 'knees' they touch their knees. When she says, 'sausages' they have to run and stand in a line, one behind the other with their hands on the shoulders of the child in front, like a string of sausages.

(c) Parachute games
Small purpose-made parachutes provide opportunities to play games which require a great deal of cooperation. The parachute is laid out on the ground and the children take hold of the edges

29

firmly in both hands. The more adult helpers the better and they should be evenly distributed around the edge of the parachute to help the children.

Upsidaisy
Everyone counts, ONE, TWO, THREE, and on three they lift their hands so raising the parachute into the air. They must NOT let go. The parachute will fill with air and should then be lowered gently to the ground. The object of the game is to get everyone lifting at the same time.

Making Waves
Everyone starts by holding the parachute in both hands. By moving the arms slowly up and down ripples can be made in the parachute. When the teacher calls, 'rough sea' big ripples are made by moving the arms faster and more vigorously. The teacher then calls, 'calm sea' and the movements become smoother.

Bouncing Teddy
A teddy bear is placed in the middle of the parachute. Everyone holds the parachute as before. By moving the parachute up and down, filling it with air, the teddy bear can be lifted up into the air. It requires close cooperation, everyone must lift at the same time.

Under the Bridge
The parachute is raised as before. Whilst it is in the air the teacher calls out the names of two children. They have to let go of the parachute and change places by running under the parachute before it comes down. Once the children understand what to do several names can be called out and they can all change places at the same time.

Making an Igloo
The parachute is raised as in 'Upsidaisy'. Once it is in the air the children take a step forward and sit down. As they do so they pull the parachute down behind them and sit on it so that they are inside it like being in an igloo. They can then chant nursery rhymes, play simple games like 'I Spy' or listen to a short story.

Buzzing Bees
The teacher outside the 'igloo' says the poem:
'Here is the beehive where are the bees?
Hidden away where nobody sees.
But soon they come creeping out of the hive,
One, two, three, four, five.'
    The children let go of the parachute and creep out one by one.

(d) Games play with unusual equipment
Children will enjoy playing with space hoppers, giant balls, car tyres etc. They will experience the sensation of being able to control something that is possibly bigger than themselves, and learn more about the forces needed in order to propel such big objects.

5 MOVEMENT TO MUSIC
It is best if music is recorded on to a cassette tape and played on a tape recorder that has numbers on it so that the start of a particular piece of music can be found quickly and easily. Children get very fidgety if they have to wait.

    The music should not be played too loudly. Children will start to move as soon as they hear the music so it is no good expecting them to wait for an introduction to be played. The fade button can be used to advantage, especially at the end or if the music needs to be stopped. The music should not be cut off in the middle of a phrase.

The music should be short and children respond well to familiar tunes. The kind of music played should be varied and a lively piece contrasted with a quiet piece, for example. Non-vocal music should be used where possible and try to avoid too much pop music. A quiet piece of music to end up with will calm the children down. Occasionally let the children listen to the music first and maybe discuss with them the kind of movements they could do to it.

The children can interpret the music freely or they can be directed but do not be too rigid or it will restrict them. They will not be able to keep strictly to the rhythm and it would be wrong to expect them to do so at this age. Some useful examples are listed below:

Fast, lively music for skipping, jumping, twirling, running.
'Lady Di' by De Senneville, played by Richard Clayderman.
'Tambourine' by Hasse, played by James Galway.

Slow dreamy music for waving the arms, turning slowly, growing up, curling down etc.
'Tubular Bells 11' by Mike Oldfield.
'The Four Seasons' by Vivaldi.

Strong loud music for stamping, big steps, stretching etc.
'Pictures at an Exhibition' by Mussorgsky, electronically created by Tomita.

Percussion instruments

Children can respond by moving to the sounds. Banging a drum will suggest marching, big steps, and stamping. Shaking a tambourine will suggest shaking movements of the hands, feet, heads, whole body. Playing a triangle will suggest slow, gentle, smooth movements, as will chime bars. Castanets will encourage fast, jerky movements.

Instruments should be played in short phrases and the children should move and 'freeze' when the sound stops.

Sounds

Children will respond to all sorts of sounds such as scraping noises, banging, crunching up paper, a bouncing ball. Body percussion means sounds made by the body such as stamping, clapping, clicking the fingers, rubbing the hands together. Children can make their own sounds to accompany their movements.

Words

These will conjure up all sorts of responses especially if they are said very slowly or very quickly. The names of different kinds of food, for example, lend themselves to a range of movements. The word 'chips' said quickly over and over again can accompany bouncy jumps and be contrasted with 'ice cream' said very slowly for slow steps.

Poems

A short poem that the children are very familiar with can be accompanied by movement. The movements can relate to the words or just fit the phrasing. It is best if each line of the poem is repeated several times so that the children have time to do the movements. For example:

Yankie Doodle came to London
Running with knees lifted high
Riding on a pony
Large steps with knees bent and the hands on the knees
He wore a feather in his cap
Walk waving the arms
And called it MACARONI
Crouch down and jump up high on the word MACARONI

(Each line is repeated four times except the last which is said only once.)

Songs

Children can move to familiar songs providing they are short. They may not have enough puff to sing and move at the same time so the teacher may have to do most of the singing. Nursery rhymes are perhaps the easiest.

Baa Baa Black Sheep

This will provide a good skipping, running, jumping rhythm.

Rock a Bye Baby

Children can find a range of ways of doing rocking actions, sitting, lying, standing, kneeling. They may be able to rock together with practise.

The planning process

Points to bear in mind when planning

Since most of the activities are experimental, the planning will evolve around providing the structure for learning to take place. This structure needs to be considered carefully to provide opportunity for all levels of ability and also to allow for progression.

Different kinds of activity will require different methods of planning.

Overall planning

The planning statement of the school or nursery will identify the needs of the children as having opportunity to learn through physical play, to explore and experiment, develop spatial awareness and other concepts, to assist growth, strength and maturation.

How this will be achieved will depend on the resources available.

Year planning

This will vary according to how the nursery is organised but differentiation between the year groups should be considered when planning to allow for development and progression.

Lesson plans

The teacher will need to plan the activities on a day to day basis in order to try to get a balance of activities during the week.

Evaluating the success of the nursery movement programme

This will require careful observation on the part of the teacher and classroom assistants. Overall responses can be observed, looking at whether the children are being 'busy' all the time, where they go and what they do. Detailed observation, in which one specific aspect is identified to be observed, should also take place regularly.

Careful records should be kept as described in chapter 7.

Chapter Three

Games in the Early Years

Introduction

Why include games in the PE programme?

There are two good reasons for including games in a physical education programme for early years' children. One is based on child development and the concept of play, and the other on the tradition of sport and games going back to prehistory.

The importance of learning through play is clearly established in chapter 2 'Laying the Foundations in the Nursery'.

A six-month-old child, in order to attract attention, will throw an object out of his pram or high chair over and over again and the game that evolves will be a kind of physical dialogue with an adult. Thus throwing as a recognized action has its roots in early infancy. Similarly a striking action is developed at an early age when a spoon is drummed on the table, a plastic peg is hammered into the hole of a construction toy, a ball is clumsily kicked or pushed with the hands along the floor.

A 2-year-old will run away from his mother chuckling with delight and she will chase after him, pick him up, swing him round and give him a big hug. This will be repeated many times and forms the basis of all chasing games which will be developed once he has achieved the locomotor skills of running, swerving and dodging.

The word 'sport', as suggested in Olivova's book 'Sport and Games in the Ancient World' is derived from the Latin *se deportare* meaning 'to amuse oneself' and from this has stemmed the concept of using the body as a form of relaxation as well as to survive by hunting, and fighting.

Sports and games, therefore, have evolved through a need to gain strength for survival together with a need to relax. Throughout history these activities have shown an unbroken continuity and many of our present sports have their roots in ancient contests which were designed to show physical strength and skills in a recreational and 'playful' context as distinct from vital competition which was necessary in order to survive.

Society today has almost eliminated the use of physical strength in order to survive and so the need to keep fit and healthy through recreation has become even more important, especially since most people have spare time on their hands and greater opportunity than ever before with the provision of sports centres and other facilities.

These two factors then, provide the justification for playing games with our children and we owe it to them to lay the foundations on which sporting skills can be built.

This can be done by teaching the basic skills required in traditional games and by playing games designed specifically for the children bridging the gap between the play concept in the nursery and the introduction of more familiar types of games in the later years of schooling.

This, therefore, is an important stage in the development of the child since,

'Until a reasonable degree of competence in the necessary skills has been acquired many traditional games not only fail to extend, but actually limit the physical capabilities of children.' (Maulden and Redfern, 1969)

Curriculum content — areas of experience children should have in games

What games skills do the children need to learn in the early years?

'Physical Education in the National Curriculum' identifies these skills at Key Stage 1 as follows:

'Pupils should be taught:
(a) Simple competitive games, including how to play them as individuals, and, when ready, in pairs and in small groups;
(b) to develop and practise a variety of ways of sending (including throwing striking, rolling and bouncing) receiving and travelling with a ball and other games equipment;
(c) elements of games play that include running, chasing, dodging, avoiding and awareness of space and other players.'

(Areas of Activity, Games)

This will best be achieved by introducing children to a range of equipment for them to play freely with and get familiar with in the reception class. They can then learn to throw and catch a bean bag, progress on to handling and kicking large balls before trying to manage a small ball. The children will be able to go on to controlling a ball with a bat. These skills are hierarchical and some children will progress at a faster rate than others so it is not possible to indicate specifically what to teach in Year 1 followed by Year 2, but knowledge of these developments will help the teacher to differentiate where appropriate.

The locomotor skills of running, swerving and dodging are different because the children are controlling their bodies rather than an object. Therefore they can be taught how to use their bodies according to the level at which they are operating.

Acquiring skill

A skill is a learned activity. It can be defined as:

'Skill is a learned ability to reproduce specific patterns of movement which achieve desired outcomes.' (Lee, 1991)

A great deal has been written about how children learn skills and the common agreement is that it depends on the input by the teacher, her motivation, guidance and instruction. The learner should have an idea of what the skill should be like and know inside himself when he has got it right.

Some ideas of how to produce these skills follows together with some simple games the children can play.

Introducing the skills of sending away and receiving (throwing and catching) using bean bags

Bean bags are easier than balls for children to handle at first because they do not bounce or roll away. Small fingers can grasp part or all the bean bag when catching.

Each task should be described verbally and accompanied with a clear demonstration by the teacher. These can be whole-class activities and are suitable for reception children. The actions need to be practised several times.

Familiarization with the bean bag

(i) Play with your bean bag and show me what you can do with it.

(ii) Put your hands out in front of your body like a tray. Place the bean bag on the tray and take it for a walk in and out of everybody.

(iii) Find a magic spot. Place your bean bag on the spot. Walk a few steps away from it watching it all the time. Run back and pick it up.

(iv) Repeat and jump away from your bean bag. Jump back and pick it up.

Sending away by sliding the bean bag along the floor

(i) Stand on your magic spot. Slide your bean bag into a space. Run and pick it up and carry it back to your magic spot.

(ii) With a partner, one bean bag between two. Stand with your feet apart making a hole. Your partner will slide the bean bag through the hole. Change over.

(iii) Can you find other ways of making a hole with your body for your partner to slide the bean bag through? (for example, putting hands on the floor as well as the feet.)

(iv) Sit on the floor facing your partner with your feet apart. Slide the bean bag to your partner.

(v) Stand beside your partner, each with a bean bag. Your partner slides the bean bag into a space. Can you hit his bean bag with your bean bag by sliding it along the floor? (Bean Bag Marbles).

(vi) Stand facing your partner. Slide the bean bag slightly to one side of him so he has to move quickly to stop it with his hands, from sliding past him.

Throwing and catching — two handed — on the spot

(i) Stand on your magic spot. Make a tray with your hands and place the bean bag on the tray. Take your hands down a little way and push the bean bag gently into the air just higher than your head. Let the bean bag drop back onto the tray. Watch the bean bag carefully all the way.

(ii) Repeat and as the bean bag falls onto your tray wrap your fingers round it and hold it tight.

(iii) Repeat and as soon as the bean bag goes up into the air make your fingers into a little cup. Catch the bean bag in the cup.

(iv) Stand facing a partner. Your partner makes a cup with his hands. Try to throw the bean bag carefully into his cup. Change over.

Throwing and catching — two handed — on the move

(i) Stand on your magic spot. Place the bean bag on a 'tray' made by your hands. Push the bean bag up into the air and a little way in front of you. Step forwards to catch it in a 'cup' made by your hands.

(ii) Repeat but push the bean bag up into the air in front and slightly to the side of you. Move quickly to catch it in a 'cup' made by your hands.

(iii) Stand facing a partner. Put the bean bag on a 'saucer' made with your hands. Push the bean bag up into the air and slightly to the side of your partner for him to move quickly and try to catch it in his 'cup'. Change over.

Throwing with one hand and catching with two

Let the children use their dominant hands. Do not encourage using the other hand at this stage.

(i) Put the bean bag in one hand. Push it up into the air and try to catch it by making a 'cup' with both hands.

(ii) Try pushing the bean bag up into the air with one hand so that you have to move quickly to catch it in both hands.

(iii) Stand facing a partner who makes a 'cup' with both hands. Try to throw the bean bag into the 'cup' with one hand. Change over.

(iv) Repeat and try to throw the bean bag slightly to the side of your partner so he has to move quickly to catch it in his 'cup'.

Throwing and catching with one hand

(i) Put the bean bag in one hand, push it up into the air, make a 'cup' with the same hand and try to catch the bean bag in the 'cup'.

(ii) Stand facing a partner. Throw the bean bag carefully to your partner with one hand so he can catch it with one hand.

To develop the throwing action the children should be given targets to aim at. These need to be designed so that the child gets a sense of achievement when he has hit the target, i.e. it falls over with a clatter. Throwing bean bags into hoops are not very motivating for the children and they quickly become bored.

Aiming at a target

This can be organized as a circuit, i.e. the children are divided into groups and each group given a different target to aim at. They then rotate from one target to the next every few minutes. Or the activities can be varied, i.e. one group can aim at a skittle, one group can practise skipping, one group can practise throwing and catching with a partner and one group play with the hoops, for example.

Hitting still targets

(i) Knock a bean bag off the top of a skittle by throwing your bean bag at it. Start close to the skittle and move back one step every time you do it.

(ii) Knock a large ball out of a quoit by throwing a bean bag at it. Stand close and throw the bean bag hard.

(iii) Put a light foam or airflow ball on a chair. Throw your bean bag at the ball and try to knock it off the chair. Count how many times you can do it.

Hitting moving targets

(i) Practise rolling a quoit along the ground.

(ii) Roll a quoit along the ground, chase after it and try to knock it over by throwing your bean bag at it.

(iii) With a partner, he rolls a large ball slowly along the ground. Try to run after it and hit it by throwing your bean bag at it. Change over.

(iv) With your partner, make up a game trying to hit a moving target. Use a bean bag and one other piece of equipment such as a quoit, skittle, ball, rope or hoop. Give your game a name.

(v) Teach your game to a different partner.

Introducing the skills of sending away, retrieving and travelling with, using large balls

Once the children are able to throw and catch bean bags fairly competently they can progress on to using large balls, probably in Year 1.

A ball measuring 15–20 cms in diameter is best. It needs to be well pumped up so that it bounces easily. The children should have one each.

Familiarization with the large ball

(i) Play with your ball and show me what you can do with it.

(ii) Take your ball for a walk by placing it on the ground and rolling it along, in and out of each other, using one hand.

(iii)   Repeat but try to place your hand behind the ball to roll it and on top of the ball to stop it rolling too far away.

(iv)   Repeat but kick the ball with your foot instead of using your hand.

(v)   Repeat using the inside of your foot and putting your foot on the ball to stop it rolling too far away. Try to keep your head above the ball all the time.

(vi)   Half the class stands still with their feet apart. The rest roll their balls using the hands, through six pairs of legs. Change over.

(vii)   Repeat but kick the ball through six pairs of legs. Change over.

(viii) Stand facing a partner, roll the ball backwards and forwards to each other. Stop the ball by putting your hand on it before you roll it back.

(ix)   Repeat but kick the ball to each other. Stop the ball as it comes to you by putting your foot on it before you kick it back.

Bouncing the ball

(i)   Stand on a magic spot holding the ball out in front of you. Place your hands either side of the ball and have your arms fairly straight.

Drop your ball and catch it again by placing your hands on either side of it. Do this several times.

(ii)   Repeat but instead of catching the ball put your hands on top of it as it bounces back up and gently push it back down again. Hands should be curved to fit around the surface of the ball. Do this several times.

(iii)   How many times can you pat bounce the ball without moving off your magic spot?

(iv)   Repeat but pat bounce the ball slightly ahead of you so that you have to move to pat bounce it next time. How many times can you pat bounce the ball on the move?

(v)   Stand facing a partner. Bounce the ball to

your partner. Try to bounce it in the middle between you. Catch the ball by placing your hands on either side of it.

(iv)   Repeat but put a hoop on the floor between you. Try to bounce the ball in the hoop for your partner to catch. How many times can you do this without dropping the ball?

(vii)   Can you bounce the ball slightly to one side of your partner so he has to move quickly to catch it?

Throwing and catching — two handed — on the spot

(i)   Stand on your magic spot. Make a saucer with your hands and place the ball on it. Take your hands down a little way and push the ball gently into the air just higher than your head. Let the ball drop back onto the saucer. Once it lands in your hands wrap your fingers round it and clutch the ball to your chest.

(ii)   Make a saucer with your hands but have a space between each hand. Hold the ball with your hands and push it gently up into the air as before. Catch it with your hands slightly apart, clutching it to you once you have hold of it. Remember to watch it all the time.

(iii)   Do this several times, pushing the ball up higher into the air each time.

(iv)   Stand facing a partner. Your partner makes a saucer with his hands slightly apart. Try to throw the ball carefully into his saucer. Change over.

Throwing and catching — two handed — on the move

(i)   Stand on your magic spot. Place the ball on a saucer made with your hands, have your hands slightly apart. Push the ball up into the air, slightly ahead of you so that you have to move quickly to catch it again. Do this several times, pushing the ball up further each time.

(ii)   Repeat pushing the ball slightly to one side of you. Move quickly to catch it.

(iii) Stand facing a partner. He makes a saucer with his hands and has them slightly apart. Throw the ball carefully a little way to the side of your partner so he has to move quickly to catch it. Change over.

Aiming at a target

Various activities can be set up in a circuit as for the bean bag work, for example.

(i)   With a partner bounce a ball in a hoop placed on the floor for him to catch.

(ii)   In threes — one holding a hoop out to the side at shoulder height, vertically. The other two throw and catch the ball so it goes through the hoop each time. Change over after three goes.

(iii) Throw a ball at a bean bag balanced on top of a cone and try to knock it off. Move back one step each time you do it.

(iv)   Roll a quoit along the floor. Run after it and try to knock it over by throwing a ball at it.

(v)   Throw a ball against a wall. Let it bounce and then catch it. How many times can you do it before you drop it. Try to hit the same spot on the wall each time.

(vi)   One child spins a hoop. The rest try to throw and catch their balls as many times as they can before the hoop stops spinning.

Practising the kicking action in a circuit

(i)   Dribble with the feet in and out of six cones placed in a line, one metre apart. When you get to the end of the line kick the ball into a 'goal' made of two cones, placed one metre apart.

(ii)   In twos, one tries to kick the ball into goal which is guarded by his partner. He tries to stop it by smothering it with his hands. He could be kneeling down to make it easier. Three goes and change over.

(iii) In twos, one dribbles the ball a little way and then kicks it to his partner who traps it. He then does the same going back the other way.

(iv)   In a group of four, one stands in the middle and kicks the ball to one of the others. The receiver stops the ball by trapping it (putting his foot on it) and then kicks it back. If the receiver misses it, he changes place with the one in the middle.

Introducing the skills of sending away and retrieving using small balls

Children can progress on to using small balls once they can throw and catch large balls reasonably competently. This will probably be towards the end of Year 1 and the beginning of Year 2 depending on how experienced they are at handling a ball. Old tennis balls are probably the easiest for them to handle providing they bounce accurately. There are other similar balls on the market, such as sorbo balls, however research has shown that children find airflow balls extremely difficult to catch as they are too light.

It is recommended that these skills are mastered out of doors if possible as small balls tend to go further than the large ones and are more difficult to control.

Familiarization with the small ball

(i)   Play with your ball and show me what you can do with it.

(ii)   Stand on a magic spot. Roll your ball into a space, chase after it, pick it up and walk back to your magic spot.

(iii) Repeat, but try to overtake the ball, turn face it, bend your knees and then scoop it up with your fingers. (Give a clear demonstration.)

Bouncing the ball

(i)   Stand on a magic spot holding the ball in one hand out in front of you. Drop it and try to catch it in two hands.

(ii) Repeat but try to catch it in one hand. Do this several times.

(iii) Repeat but instead of catching the ball pat bounce it back down again using one hand only, try to hit the ball at the top of the bounce or just as it starts falling back down.

(iv) How many times can you pat bounce the ball without moving off your magic spot? If the ball rolls away pick it up and start again.

(v)   Pat bounce the ball slightly ahead of you so you have to move to pat bounce it next time. How many times can you pat bounce it on the move?

(vi) Stand facing a partner. Bounce the ball carefully to him for him to catch. Try to bounce it in the middle between you. Catch the ball in two hands and bounce it with one. How many times can you do this without dropping it?

(vii) Can you bounce the ball slightly to one side of your partner so he has to move to catch it?

(viii) Repeat task (vi) then task (vii) using one hand only to bounce and catch the ball.

(ix) Stand closer to your partner. Bounce the ball to him and he will pat bounce it back to you. How many times can you pat bounce the ball to each other? Remember to hit the ball at the top of the bounce or as it starts to fall.

Throwing and catching

(i) Stand on your magic spot. Make a saucer with your hands and place the ball on it, take your hands down a little way and push the ball gently up into the air just higher than your head. Let the ball drop back on to the saucer. Once it lands in your hands wrap your fingers round the ball and clutch it to your chest. Remember to watch it all the time.

(ii) Repeat and push the ball higher into the air each time. Make a cup with your fingers and get the cup under the ball so that it drops into it. Watch the ball all the time.

(iii) Repeat but push the ball slightly ahead of you so that you have to move to catch it.

(iv) Stand on your magic spot. Throw the ball up into the air using one hand and catch it in both hands.

(v) Repeat but throw the ball up slightly ahead of you so that you have to move to catch it. How many times can you do this without dropping the ball?

(vi) Stand on your magic spot. Throw the ball

up into the air with one hand and catch it in one hand.

(vii) Can you throw the ball with one hand and catch it in the other?

(viii) Repeat task (vi) and (vii) on the move.

(ix) Stand in a big space on a magic spot. Throw the ball as far as you can. Run after it, pick it up and come back to your magic spot.

(x) Repeat, but throw the ball OVERARM. (Teacher or child to demonstrate.)

Throwing and catching with a partner

(i) Stand facing your partner fairly close together. Place the ball on a saucer made by your two hands and push the ball towards him so he can catch it in a cup made by his two hands.

(ii) Move further apart. How many times can you do this without dropping the ball?

(iii) Throw the ball to your partner using one hand, for him to catch in both hands. How many times can you do this?

(iv) Throw the ball to your partner using one hand for him to catch in one hand. How many times can you do this without dropping the ball?

(v) Throw the ball slightly to one side of your partner so he has to move quickly to catch it.

Aiming at a target

Various activities can be set up in a circuit. Some activities could be using a bean bag, some using large balls and some using small balls, for example:

(i) Throw a small ball to knock a bean bag off the top of a skittle. Place the skittle in front of a wall so that if you miss the target the ball will not roll too far away. Try throwing overarm and underarm, which is best?

(ii)   Roll a quoit along the ground, chase after it and try to knock it over by throwing a small ball at it. Try to throw overarm.

(iii) Aim at a high target such as a chalk mark on a wall, a netball ring or a team band tied to some stop netting. Move further away each time you hit the target. Try to throw overarm.

Introducing the skills of sending away and retrieving using a play bat and a ball

In the first instance the hand should be used as a bat and then a play bat, or table tennis bat should be used. Racquets with long handles are too difficult for the children to manipulate at this stage. Tennis balls are probably the best size for the children, although a slightly larger ball may be easier for any child having difficulties. Shuttlecocks are also useful for children having difficulties as they stay in the air longer and do not roll away.

Using the hand as a bat

(i)   Stand on your magic spot. Place the ball on your hand and pat it up a little way into the air keeping your hand flat. How many times can you do this?

(ii)   Pat bounce your ball using your hand, try to keep your hand flat.

(iii) Repeat tasks 1 and 2 but move about as you do it.

(iv)   Alternatively pat your ball up, let it drop and then pat bounce it.

(v)   Make up a pattern patting your ball up and pat bouncing it, for example, pat it up once, let it drop and then pat bounce it three times.

(vi)   Teach your pattern to a partner and learn his pattern.

(vii) Can you do your pattern and then your partner's without stopping?

(viii) Sit facing a partner, pat your ball to him along the ground using your hand and he will pat it back to you.

(ix)   Make up a 'batting' game based on task (viii). Remember to give your game a name.

(x)   Find a new partner and teach him your game. Learn his game.

Using a play bat

All the above tasks can be repeated using a play bat instead of the hand. Explain that the bat is like a BIG hand and show the children how to hold the bat with the fingers gripped tightly around the handle.

The children can start with trying to balance the ball on the bat whilst standing still and then whilst moving about.

They can then progress on to batting the ball to each other, i.e.:

(i)   Face a partner who has a bat. Bounce the ball to him. He will bat it back to you for you to catch in both hands. Do this five times and then change over.

(ii)   Repeat but try to catch the ball in one hand.

(iii) Repeat but bounce the ball slightly to one side of him so he has to move quickly to pat it back to you.

(iv)   Using a bat, pat bounce the ball to your partner who will pat bounce it back to you. How many times can you do this?

(v)   If a wall is available — hit the ball against the wall, our partner will let it bounce and then he will hit it against the wall.

(vi)   Stand one on either side of a bench, or a cane placed on two skittles. Hit the ball carefully over the bench or cane to your partner. He will let it bounce before hitting it back over the bench or cane and then you will do the same. How many times can you do this?

These skills can be incorporated into a skills circuit as previously mentioned.

Children can make up their own 'How many' type games, for example:

How many times can you pat bounce the ball whilst your partner skips twenty times using a rope?

Some class games to play with the children using these skills

Using bean bags: HOOPLA

Each child has a hoop and a bean bag. The hoops are placed side by side in a circle and each child stands inside a hoop, holding his bean bag. Four hoops, one of each colour are placed in the centre of the circle. The children run round the outside of the hoops and when the teacher calls out, 'Stop' they stand in the hoop nearest to them. The teacher then gives instructions such as, 'Those with yellow bean bags throw them into the yellow hoop.' This followed by blue, green and red bean bags being thrown into the corresponding hoops. They then count up to see which hoop has the most bean bags in it.

The children retrieve their bean bags when told to do so. The game is repeated but instead of running round the hoops a different action is chosen, for example, hopping, skipping or jumping. Different colours can also be chosen, for example, 'Those with yellow bean bags throw them into the green hoop.'

Using large balls: BIG FRIENDLY GIANT

The children stand in a circle and the teacher stands in the middle. She throws a ball to a child at random, for him to catch. If he catches it he takes a step backwards and then throws the ball back to the teacher. Any child clever enough to end up three steps away, becomes a big friendly giant. If he is skilful enough he can replace the teacher.

Using small balls: WANDERING JACK

The children are in four teams and stand side by side in a square facing the centre. A line is drawn in front of each team. A large ball (Jack) is placed in the centre. On a signal from the teacher, the children aim their balls at Jack and try to knock him over one of the other teams' lines without letting it cross their line. They may retrieve any ball which comes their way but must not cross the line. These can then be thrown at Jack. Jack must not be touched by hand. As soon as Jack crosses a line the game is stopped and all the balls retrieved. The team whose line has been crossed loses a life.

Running actions

'Pupils should be taught elements of games play that include running, chasing, dodging, avoiding and awareness of space and other players.' (National Curriculum Physical Education, 1995)

Children need opportunities to run on as many occasions as possible. They seldom, these days, have the chance to experience the thrill of running for its own sake, being escorted and supervised at all times because of security.

Reception children will not run far, stopping frequently to ascertain that an adult is close by and they prefer to change from running to skipping to hopping, pausing to inspect something they have seen, taking a breath before going off again.

Year 1 children can be introduced to running with good style and Year 2 children are ready to build up their stamina.

Children can be taught to run with the arms bent up, fists loosely clenched with their thumbs on top. The arms help to drive the body along and if an increase in speed is needed then the arms can be 'pumped' forwards and backwards at a faster rate and the legs automatically will follow.

The legs propel the body along and the children should be aware of the slight knee lift. The weight should be forwards over the balls of the feet and the heels barely touching the ground. The children should not be told to run on their toes as this is almost impossible, especially when running fast.

The head should be held straight and the children must look where they are going.

Never let the children run towards a wall in case they have difficulty in stopping.

Swerving and dodging

Children need to be aware of how the body can lean in order to swerve. This can be related to the ways the body is used when riding a bicycle in order to steer. To get through a small space they can be taught to turn the shoulders and lead with the side of the body.

They should be introduced to the different length of paces, for example, when in a big space they can take big steps, but when they are in little spaces they need to take little steps and they can practise being nimble by taking a series of irregular little steps in all directions.

In order to dodge they should be shown how to push away on one foot and take a step in a new direction.

A distinction between running straight 'round the room' and swerving 'in and out' of each other needs to be apparent.

At all times children must be taught not to run with the arms out in front of them ready to push other children out of the way.

Stopping

Children need to be able to stop suddenly with control both on a signal from the teacher and on impulse, for safety considerations.

A warning from the teacher should be given, such as 'and . . . stop!' Children should be taught to 'freeze' with one foot in front of the other, acting as a brake. The arms are bent up, and all muscles gripped tightly. The knees are slightly bent to lower the centre of gravity.

Introducing running actions

(i) Run quietly round the room.
(ii) Run in and out of each other.

(iii) Run and stop on signal.
(iv) Run slowly round the room, run faster when told, slow down when told.
(v) Run taking long strides, change to taking little steps.
(vi) Run forwards, stop on signal, change to running backwards. (Look over the shoulder to see where you are going.)
(vii) Play 'follow my leader' = teacher as leader.
(viii) Repeat task (vii) — choose a child as leader.

Chasing games

Many children put into a chasing game fail to understand the nature of the game and appear lost and bewildered. Therefore games need to be structured and concepts introduced gradually.

Language

There are various terms used to describe the chaser which may be puzzling to a child at first. It is insufficient to say 'You're IT' or 'You're ON' unless every child understands the implications of the phrase. We tend to take these terms for granted. How can we explain what we mean to children?

Being chased

This is possibly the first fun activity a child might be involved in. He runs away from his mother, inviting her to chase after him, knowing she will catch up with him and gather him into her arms.

> 'The infant who, relishing escape but anticipating capture, dashes away from his mother as she follows in mock pursuit, epitomises the spirit and form of a game, his action is spontaneous and rewarding.' (DES, 1972)

Being caught

This is a very old tradition. Being touched and turned into stone, gold, a handsome prince etc. goes back to early civilizations and provides the material for many a myth and legend.

> 'In chasing games a touch with the tip of the finger is enough to transform a player's part in the game. It is as if the chaser was evil, or magic, or diseased, and his touch was contagious.' (Opie, 1969)

A chasing game involves children trying to avoid being touched by the chaser. 'Touching' activities can be introduced to help the child understand this concept. He also needs to know when he is touched. If approached from behind he may not feel the touch and be unaware that he has been caught.

Some chasing games to play with the children using running actions

Lego

The teacher calls out, 'Touch your knees' for example, and the children have to run in and out of each other with their hands on their knees. Or she might call, 'Touch your heads' and then they would have to run in and out with their hands on their heads. If she calls out, 'Lego' they have to stand facing another child with their hands on their partner's legs.

Copy cat

In twos, one child copies exactly what the other child does. When the teacher calls out, 'Copy cat' they run and find a new partner and stand with their hands touching, palms uppermost.

Busy Bee

Children run in and out of each other. When the teacher calls out, 'Busy Bee' they quickly find a partner. The teacher then calls out, 'Feet to feet', for example, and each pair has to stand with their feet touching. This is followed by other instructions such as, 'Arm to arm', 'Back to back' etc. When the teacher calls out 'Busy Bee' they run and find a new partner.

Tom and Gerry

The children are in pairs. One is called Tom and the other Gerry. When the teacher calls, 'Tom', Tom chases Gerry, but does not actually catch him. When the teacher calls out, 'Gerry' then Gerry chases Tom.

Catch my tail

The chaser tucks a team band into his waistband at the back. The other children try to snatch the team band without being touched by the chaser. If touched they have to 'freeze'. Whoever snatches the team band becomes the new chaser.

Keeper of the keys

Children sit in a circle, leaving a large space which is the 'castle door'. The keeper of the castle keys is a child who sits in the middle with his eyes closed, asleep. On the floor behind the keeper are his keys. (This can be a bunch of keys or a bean bag.)

The teacher chooses a child who creeps up to the keys, rattles them, puts them down and then runs out through the 'door'. The keeper wakes up and chases after him. He runs round the circle and back through the 'door'. If he gets there without being caught by the keeper he becomes the new keeper. If not he sits down in the circle and the keeper goes back to sleep.

Other considerations

(i) Teachers should try to pair off children with similar abilities so that a slower child is not trying to chase a really fast child. Obviously a fast child needs the opportunity to use his skills and should not be penalized, but it can become very frustrating for the chaser if he stands no chance of catching him.

(ii)   All games should be given a name, so that the next time they are played the children recognize them and this saves going through all the rules again. A brief resumé will be necessary for those who have forgotten the rules.

(iii)   When introducing a game give a clear demonstration together with a verbal explanation, if necessary breaking it down and teaching it bit by bit.

The teaching process

Playing games with children

Children love playing simple games and, as well as mastering basic skills, they need the opportunity to understand what a game is all about, and the purpose of it.

The DES Curriculum Matters Booklet, *Physical Education from 5 to 16* published in 1989 states that by the age of 7 children should have had experiences which enable them to . . .

'play simple games with, and alongside, others and with simple rules of their own and the teacher's devising, thereby experiencing membership of a team.'

It goes on to say . . .

'The major emphasis for young children should be on sharing and working together. But the fun of simple competition should not be denied to them . . .

Any game with a team, however small, is about cooperation as well as competition; both elements need to be stressed so that the manner of taking part depends on skill, teamwork and the acceptance of rules . . .

Inventing games involves children in working cooperatively to agree some or all the circumstances in which their play takes place, for example, how points or goals are scored, the composition of teams, the equipment to be used, the shape and extent of the playing area . . .

The games children play at this stage should have teams and playing areas which are small enough to ensure maximum involvement and to keep the problems associated with 'reading' the game at a level with which they can cope and experience success and satisfaction.'

So often children are put into a game situation and appear totally bewildered with what is going on. To cope with this they either opt out all together, or respond in a completely different way from that which is intended. A few, of course, will understand straight away.

Therefore we need to introduce the children to all that is involved in a gradual and progressive way. The implications of being part of a team, understanding how to interpret rules, the complexities of tactics and strategies used in a game, and making sense of the ways of scoring all need to be carefully thought out and presented to the children in a challenging and stimulating way.

Children cannot be thrown 'in at the deep end' into a game of rounders, football or netball in the later years without the basic understanding having been fully grasped.

All these concepts can be taught through the playing of simple games which are not dependent on a high level of skill. They need to be taught *alongside* the appropriate skills required.

Introducing children to being part of a team

In the first instance children need to have the opportunity of 'playing together' and to experience the cooperative feeling of belonging to the class or group. Activities or games in which they come to know that 'this is what we do' need to be introduced in the nursery and carried on through the reception class. There are many traditional singing, action and circle games that fit into this category, many of which are, sadly, dying out.

From this children can begin to play games in which one child assumes a different role from the rest. Some of the 'chanting' games fall into this category, such as 'What's the Time, Mr Wolf?' The idea that the class can form two groups instead of just the one, can be introduced by playing games in which half the class assumes a different role from the other. Here we have both the cooperative element and the competition aspect of one group trying to outwit the other in some way.

The children are now ready to pay attention to different formations the teams can assume. Getting into groups unaided, forming lines and circles, being generally aware of where other members of the team are, all have a vital part to play in a game.

However, these complex relationships cannot be understood if the children are also having to master the difficult skills of catching and throwing etc. So we need to keep the skill level very basic.

Playing by the rules

All games have rules so from the very start we are explaining 'this is what you have to do'. But the way children are introduced to these rules is often very haphazard and confusing to many of them. Teachers often complain that the children do not listen and do not do what they are told.

The safety factor is always of paramount importance and so the rules we give children in physical education are mainly to do with control. In the first instance children need to be able to run and stop safely so many of the games we play in this category are based on stopping on command. Children must learn to avoid

crashing into each other and games can specifically be played to help them with this.

When we first start playing games with children they are unable to pay attention to where they go as well as the business of the game itself. Children beginning to play netball, for example, are so busy looking where the ball is, they are unable to look at the ground to see the lines on the court. So we need to introduce rules that focus on looking for and keeping to boundaries such as hoops, lines, and circles.

Other rules are made to determine the nature of the game. For older children games fall into categories such as invasive games in which one team invades the territory of the other, as in netball and football. Or the game can be played over a net as in tennis and badminton. The third category of games includes the running games such as cricket and rounders in which a player has to run a specific distance in order to score.

For most infants these categories are inappropriate although teachers need to be aware of their existence and prepare the way for the children in readiness for games in the junior school.

The method of scoring is also determined by the rules. In adult games this can be very confusing to the uninitiated. Compare the methods of scoring in net games. For example, badminton, table tennis, volley ball and tennis, all have very different methods of scoring. More arguments will arise from children playing games unsupervised through the scoring than anything else.

Children need to be introduced gradually to how points and goals are scored and again, as in other elements of trying to make sense of the format, the skill content needs to be kept simple. Children find it difficult to 'do' and count at the same time.

Tactics and strategies involved in playing a game

Many concepts overlap and are difficult to separate out. By focussing on one aspect we can simplify things for children and the results will be more rewarding for them and the teacher.

We can play games with the children where the emphasis is on the concepts of 'in and out', and 'on and off'.

We need to play games where the making and creating of spaces is the most important factor as this is one of the most crucial elements to many adult major games played in this country.

The surprise element, and being faced with unpredictable situations in which decisions have quickly to be taken, also play a vital part in playing games. This is the exciting element of a game, not knowing what is going to happen and trying to anticipate the moves in readiness. Relays and games where each child takes it in turn to perform an action do not allow for this quick decision making and do not help in judging, reading the game, or planning in advance.

Details of games that can be played with the children under these headings are given below.

Teachers can make up games for their own classes based on whatever aspect they feel the children need to develop. In order for a game to be successful it needs an appealing title, clear simple rules, a progression, i.e. one thing happens and then as a result something else happens, an element of unpredictability and a decisive outcome. Elimination games should not be played at this stage.

Games to play with the children to help them understand what is involved

Animal Magic — A game played all together

The children all find a 'magic spot' and stand on it. They then hop in and out of each other saying:

> 'Some little frogs went hopping one day,
> Over the hills and far away.
> When they knew it was time for tea,
> They all came hopping back to me'

On the last word they should arrive back on their magic spots.

The poem is repeated with the following words replacing the first line:

> 'Some little ducks went swimming one day
> Some little snakes went sliding one day
> Some little horses went trotting one day'

The children do the appropriate actions and change the word in the last line from hopping to whatever action they are doing.

The Outback — A game in which one child plays a different role from the rest

One child is a dingo. The rest are kangaroos. The dingo tries to catch the kangaroos. When a kangaroo is caught he curls up on the spot. Another kangaroo comes along and puts him in his pouch (i.e. he stands behind him and cuddles him). The game ends when the dingo gives up or all the baby kangaroos are in their pouches.

Tadpole — A game in which half the class does something different from the rest

Half the class forms a circle. This represents the body of a tadpole. The rest form a line. They are the tail of the tadpole. The body of the tadpole passes a ball around the circle as many times as they can. At the same time, each child in turn in the tail of the tadpole runs around the body. The last one to run round calls out stop. The number of times the ball has been passed around the circle is announced. The teams change over and the new body has to try to beat the previous score.

Playing by the rules

Rainbow

Different coloured hoops, one for each child, are scattered about the room. The children run anywhere but do not enter a hoop. The teacher calls out a colour and the children have to stand in a hoop of that colour.

Not more than two children are allowed to stand in one hoop, anyone unable to get into a hoop has to run and stand behind the teacher. The last child in the line stays with the teacher and tells her which colour to call out next time.

Octopus

One child is the fisherman. The rest are fish. The children run anywhere and if a child is caught by the fisherman he has to stand still and become an octopus. He can use his arms to try to catch other fish. When an octopus catches a fish, he must stand behind him and also become part of the octopus. The first octopus to get all its eight arms is the winner.

Helping the children to make up their own games

Children enjoy making up their own games. They are taking the responsibility for their own learning and are becoming aware of what is involved in a game. They learn to experiment, select and perfect an idea and the decision making process gives them greater understanding of the nature of a game.

It is best if the teacher gives the children a starting point, such as, 'Sit facing your partner with your legs out wide, and using a bean bag, try to find a way to slide it to hit your partner's legs without letting it hit your legs. Give your game a name.'

Having made up a simple game with a partner, the pair can split up and teach a new partner how to play. He can learn the partner's game. In this way the children will be introduced to a variety of games made up by themselves.

Games can be written down using a simple format. These can be printed out on a computer and laminated so that the children can perhaps choose a game to lay at playtime or in a lesson.

The children could make their own book of games perhaps.

Starting points:

(i)   'Hot' stands with his back to his partner with his feet apart. Using a large ball, make up a game in which 'Cold' has to get the ball through 'Hot's' legs. Give your game a name.

(ii) Place a hoop on the ground between you. Make up a game in which a ball has to bounce in the hoop. Give your game a name.

(iii) Place a rope on the ground. 'Hot' stands on one side and 'Cold' stands on the other. You may not cross the rope. Make up a game using a large ball.

(iv) 'Hot' and 'Cold' each choose a different piece of equipment. Make up a game using both pieces. Give your game a name.

(v)   Make up a game in which a hoop has to be bowled along the ground. Give your game a name.

Examples of games made up by Year 2 children

(i)

Our game is called:	*Throw Hoop*
Number who can play:	Three girls, three boys
What we used:	One hoop, one skittle
Rules:	Throw the hoop and if you miss the skittle you step forward one step. If you get the hoop on the skittle move back one step. If you get the hoop on the skittle all the time you get fifteen points. If you lose all the time you get 0 points.

When you do this game you take turns. The end.

Frances and Mary-Anne

* *

(ii)

Our game is called:	*Punch Ball*
Number who can play:	Six
What we used:	Ball
Rules:	If you punch the ball you get three points If you miss the ball you lose your points.

Tom, Jack and Ben

* *

(iii)

Our game is called:	*Cone and ball*
Number who can play:	Two
What we used:	Two cones and a ball
Rules:	You have to hold a cone up and the other person tries to get the ball in the cone. If you get the ball in the cone it is the other person's go.

Mandy and Lucy

* *

(iv)

Our game is called:	*Hit the Ring*
Number who can play:	Two
What we used:	We used a cone and a ball and a ring
Rules:	You have to knock down the ring and if you knock down the ring you get 10 points and if you both hit the ring you both get some points.

Alexander and Jael

* *

(v) Our game is called: *Scooper*

Number who can Play: Four

What we used: Hoops and balls

Rules: Not to roll it;
Not too high;
And play fair.
Throw the ball in the spinning hoop to get points.
You swap over after you have thrown the ball.

Aaron and Joe

* *

(vi) Our game is called: *Hoopla*

Number who can play: Two upwards

What we used: Six hoops, one ball, one orange cone and three different coloured cones

Rules:
(a) You have to line the cones up in a diamond shape with the orange one at the back.
(b) Give each person 3 hoops and they have to throw them onto the cones.
(c) The cone in the front is 10 points and the cone behind on the left is 30 points and the one on the right is 50 points and the one at the back is 100 points.
(d) The one who wins is the person who gets the most points.

Fiona and Sammy

* *

(vii) Our game is called: *Circular Throw*

Number who can play: Two

What we used: Ball and hoop

Rules:
(a) One person gets the hoop and spins it round.
(b) The other person tries to throw the ball through the hoop.
(c) If you can't get through have another go and you lose a point.
(d) If you get it through you get two points. Then you pass it to the next person.

Kirsty and Hannah

* *

These games were made up by class 2 at Rodmell Primary School with the help of Chloe Phillips, a student at the University of Brighton in March 1993.

Ways to help children make up their own games

Once the children have learnt to cooperate and compete with a partner, then activities in which one pair competes against another can be introduced.

These can take the form of 'How many?' type games such as, 'How many times can "Hot" and "Cold" throw the ball to each other, whilst 'Hat' and "Coat" take it in turns to run round two cones, placed three metres apart?'

The concept of passing a ball and trying to intercept a pass can develop. For example, two goals are made five metres apart. 'Hot' and 'Cold' try to get the ball into one goal and 'Hat' and 'Coat' into the other goal. The ball must be rolled along the ground.

Children can make up their own games along the same lines using similar starting points, for example:

> Place a rope on the ground stretched out in a line. 'Hot' and 'Cold' stand one side, and 'Hat' and 'Coat' stand the other side. Make up a game in which a large ball has to bounce on either side of the line. Give your game a name.

'Hot' and 'Cold' pass a ball to each other. 'Hat' and 'Coat' try to get it. What happens next?

Once children have made up their games and had an opportunity to play their own and others' games, they should have a chance to evaluate them. The games will, in fact, evolve, being adapted, altered, and added to as they are being played. Children make up games whilst playing on their own at home and will verbalize the rules, but in fact not keep to them. This does not seem to worry them, and it can so happen that two children can play the same game, each playing to a different set of rules.

In this way we are involving the children in the CONTINUOUS PROCESS of physical education, namely PLANNING, PERFORMING AND EVALUATING, as outlined in the general programme of study in the National Curriculum Physical Education document.

Games to help children to 'find a partner'

In order to get the children to mix up when working with a partner, some simple games can be played. The teacher has to decide whether it is more important to pair the children off according to ability, friendships, ages, if in a mixed-age class, or even size. By playing simple games, the children can be paired off at random thus helping them to learn to play with whoever they find themselves.

Younger children take a long time to 'find a partner' and will often choose one and then discard him in favour of another, so a different tactic may need to be applied to avoid rejection, and speed up the process.

Older children will cling to a firm friend and not work with a child they know less well. Nearly every class has a child who is left without a partner and so this situation needs careful handling. If there is an odd number in the class the teacher has to decide either to join in, in which case she cannot watch the others, or a group of three has to be created which in turn presents a problem. This can only be resolved by the teacher who knows her children well.

Children finding themselves without a partner must not be excluded from the activity.

Games which involve finding a partner

Cups and Saucers

Half the class are 'cups' and make 'handles' by putting one hand on the waist. The rest are 'saucers' and make shapes like saucers by putting both hands on the waist.

The 'saucers' stand still in a space.

The 'cups' run in and out of the 'saucers'.

When the teacher calls out 'cups and saucers' each 'cup' stands beside a 'saucer' linking arms.

Caribbean Handshake

Children run in and out of each other. When the teacher calls out, 'now' they stop and face another child nearest to them. One child holds his hands out in front of him and the other gently slaps his hands on top. They change over hands and as they do so they say 'hello'.

Up the Garden Path

Children run in and out of each other as if in a garden. The teacher calls out, 'freeze'. They all stay still on the spot. The teacher says, 'The flowers are growing', and each child reaches out one hand and holds another child's hand who is near to him without moving his feet if possible. The children then walk round the garden holding hands with their partners.

Children remember what to do in a game if they are given names that appeal to them. Rather than distinguish between girls and boys, it is better to use recognized pairs such as, 'cups' and 'saucers', 'hot' and 'cold', 'bears' and 'monkeys'. The children will be able to make suggestions of names for pairings of their own, or topical names from stories they have been reading could be used.

Classification of games

The accepted classification of games (i.e. invasion, net/wall, fielding games) is not appropriate for early years' children, chasing games being the nearest to invasive games that they are most likely to encounter, however, some teachers feel that net games should be introduced in Year 2, and so a brief outline of how this could be done follows.

Net games

In the first instance children need to understand the concept of over and under in this context. This can be done by activities such as:

    step over and slide under various objects;
    throw a ball high into the air;
    roll a ball under a cane balanced on two cones.

This can be developed by introducing a partner and working cooperatively:

    slide a beanbag through your partner's legs;
    throw a ball over a line to your partner;

throw a ball through a hoop supported on activity skittles to your partner;
bounce a ball over a cane balanced on two cones to your partner; throwing objects, (quoits, large balls etc.) over a high net or rope to a partner.

Children can be introduced to bat and ball skills by:

    working individually batting a ball against a wall;
    in twos, letting a ball bounce and hitting it alternatively;
    keeping a rally going by hitting a ball over a line to a partner, who lets it bounce and then hits it back;
    keeping a rally going and introducing simple scoring of their own devising, hitting the ball over a cane balanced on two cones.

The planning process

Points to bear in mind when planning

(i)   Research (Cooper, 1977) has shown that when a teacher directs the learning process, children make greater progress and are more motivated than if they are left to discover and find out for themselves. Regular, carefully planned sessions will improve the children's confidence and enjoyment.

(ii)   When learning a skill, time needs to be given for the performer to absorb the implications involved and internalise the process. This may take several lessons.

(iii) The learning of specific skills is a hierarchical process but the understanding of playing games is very complex so children need to be exposed to a range of situations across a broad spectrum.

(iv)   Children's level of performance and understanding varies widely so differentiation of tasks needs to be built in to the planning to cater for individual needs.

(v) Resources need to be adequate and readily available. Whenever possible games lessons should take place out of doors and playground markings are very useful. Grids, four metres x three metres painted on the ground enable children to have their own territory in which to play. If these are not available then boundaries can be identified by using cones, chalk, markers or even a line of beanbags. Plastic 'corners' can be purchased through Educational catalogues.

Overall planning

The needs of the children have been established as:

having opportunity to practise and improve the basic skills of sending, receiving and travelling with a ball;
running, swerving, dodging and chasing;
playing a range of games devised to help understanding;
making up games of their own to play.

How these needs will be met will be outlined in each individual school's curriculum policy statement describing the amount of time to be allocated to games, and the resources available.

Year planning

Units of work for the year need to be decided, (for example, the first half of the autumn term and the second half of the spring term) and the main focal point of each unit will contribute to the overall progression throughout the school. This makes it easier for the class teacher if she knows what work has been covered and the procedures that have already been established.

Development and consolidation through the unit of work should be apparent.

Units of work can be built up on one of four formats. The unit can be skill-based, based on understanding the nature of games, games-making or a mixture of all three.

Thus a 'master plan' can be devised.

Planning by the class teacher

The outline 'master plan' is a skeleton plan and then the lessons need to be planned in more detail. These should not be planned too far in advance because the evaluation of the first lesson will influence the content of the next lesson.

All lessons should start with a 'warming up' activity. Children need to adjust to the large space, particularly out of doors. They find it difficult to listen and focus on the teacher as she will most likely be further away from them. In the classroom most instructions are given to the children sitting on the carpet, looking up at her and fairly close to her. It is important that the children are given a simple task that will get them warm.

The development of the lesson will most likely be in two stages and depend on the unit of work.

If the unit of work is skill based then the children will begin working individually on a specific task. This may be of an exploratory nature with reception children or very directed with the older ones. The children could then go on to an activity in which the skill is applied in a partner situation, working cooperatively, or a skills circuit set up.

In a unit of work on understanding the nature of games then the children could play a game with which they are familiar and then go on to learn a new game based on the same concept.

If the unit of work is one of mixed activities then a skill could be practised, a game made up incorporating that skill or a traditional game taught to the children.

All lessons should end with equipment being put tidily away and the children calmed down by doing an action very slowly.

A list of these activities can be found at the end of chapter 1.

Evaluating the success of the games programme

In order to evaluate the games programme, teachers need to draw up criteria which can be used. As a result of this the programme can then be amended if necessary.

The criteria will need to include such factors as:

> have the children had the opportunity to use a variety of equipment?
> are they able to throw and catch a ball competently and accurately and use a play bat?
> are they able to run, swerve, dodge and play chasing games?
> have they learnt a range of class games?
> are they able to make up and play their own games?
> can they cooperate when playing games?
> can they handle simple competitive situations?

An example of a simple assessment procedure that could be used to assess individual children's progress is found on page 127.

SAMPLE UNITS OF WORK FOR EACH AGE GROUP

RECEPTION CLASSES

Sample 1

Area of Activity: Games.

Unit of Work: Introduction to a variety of equipment.

Learning Intentions: for the children to explore the nature of balls, hoops, quoits, and bean bags and discover how to handle them. They will be introduced to playing simple games all together in order to learn the elements of games play.

Development over six lessons

The lessons will begin with a simple activity that the children will do all together to learn to follow instructions and get used to the space. They will then have a free choice of equipment to play with and this will be followed by more limited choice. A simple class game will be introduced towards the end of every lesson.

(i)   Free choice of equipment.
'Follow My Leader' — the teacher will lead the children about the space.
The children will choose a piece of equipment and play with it.
The lesson will end by playing 'Oh Grandmama', (see chapter 2) followed by a quiet activity.

(ii)   Choice of equipment — hoops, large balls and skipping ropes.
'Follow My Leader' as before.
The children will choose a piece of equipment and play with it and then change it for another piece. The teacher will make suggestions as to how each piece can be used. Children will show the rest of the class some ways of using the equipment. The lesson will end with 'Oh Grandmama' followed by a quiet activity.

(iii) Choice of equipment — bean bags, small balls, play bats.
'Follow My Leader' as before.
Jumping 'on a magic spot'.
All children will choose between bean bags and bats and balls.
The teacher will make suggestions as before.
The lesson will end by playing 'Sausages' (see chapter 2) followed by a quiet activity.

(iv)   Choice of equipment — two pieces each — a hoop and a large ball.
'Follow My Leader' — the teacher will lead the children as before and then she will choose a child to be the leader.
Jumping on a magic spot.
The children will each play with a hoop and a large ball, the teacher will make

suggestions, such as, 'Can you bounce our ball in the hoop?'
The lesson will end by playing 'Sausages', followed by a quiet activity.

(v)   Choice of equipment — two pieces each — a quoit and a skipping rope.
'Follow My Leader' — a child will be the leader.
Hopping on a 'magic spot'.
The children will play with the quoits and skipping ropes, the teacher will make suggestions, such as, 'can you bowl your quoit across a line made by your skipping rope?' Children will show the others some ways of using the equipment.
The lesson will end by playing 'Oh Grandmama' and 'Sausages' followed by a quiet activity.

(vi)   Choice of equipment — two pieces each, no restrictions.
'Follow My Leader' — a child will be the leader.
Jumping and hopping on a 'magic spot'.
Children will choose any two pieces of equipment and play with it.
The lesson will end by playing 'Oh Grandmama' and 'Sausages', followed by a quiet activity.

Criteria for the evaluation of this unit of work

(i)   Have the children experienced a range of equipment to play with?

(ii)   How did they cope when faced with a limited choice of equipment?

(iii) Were they able to play 'Follow My Leader' when
(a)   the teacher was the leader?
(b)   when a child was the leader?

(iv)   How successful have the games been?

(v)   Does anything need to be changed?

Sample 2
Area of Activity: Games.
Unit of Work: Chasing Games.
Relevant National Curriculum PE Statement:
pupils should be taught elements of games play

that include chasing, dodging, avoiding and awareness of space and other players.

Learning Intentions: to improve running actions, to understand the concept of chasing and being chased.

Development over six lessons

The lessons will start with running activities to improve the skill. The children will be introduced to a range of chasing games.

(i)   Running and stopping
        Children will practise running in and out of each other.
        They will learn to stop on a given signal. The children will play 'Lego'. They will then play 'What's the Time, Mr Wolf?'
        The lesson will end with running slowly in and out of each other.

(ii)   Running and swerving
        The lesson will start by a recap on running and stopping.

The children will learn how to swerve to avoid each other.

The children will play 'Lego' and 'Copy Cat'.

The lesson will end by playing 'What's the Time, Mr Wolf?' and walking slowly in and out of each other.

(iii)   Awareness of space
        Children will practise running in and out of each other, stopping and swerving as before.
        They will identify a 'magic spot' and run away from and to it on a given signal.
        They will play, 'Animal Magic'.
        They will play 'Lego' and 'Copy Cat.'
        They will end the lesson by jogging around the playground.

(iv)   Awareness of space — continued
        Children will run in and out of each other in large spaces and close together in small spaces, without touching.

They will identify their 'magic spots' as before.

They will play, 'Animal Magic.'

They will learn to play 'The Outback' game.

The lesson will end with the children jumping up and down quietly on their magic spots.

(v) Chasing each other

Children will play 'Follow My Leader' in small groups.

Children will follow a partner, copying his movements and where he goes.

Children will learn to play 'Tom and Gerry'.

The lesson will end with a game of 'What's the Time, Mr Wolf?'

The children will follow the teacher who leads them quietly back to the classroom.

(vi) Consolidation

Children will practise all their running, stopping and swerving skills.

They will choose which games they want to play, from all the games they have learnt during this unit of work.

The lesson will end with the children walking quietly in and out of each other.

Criteria for the evaluation of this unit of work

(i) Has the children's ability to run safely and competently improved?

(ii) Have they learnt how to dodge, avoid others and use the space well?

(iii) Have they understood the concept of chasing and being chased?

(iv) How successful have the games been?

(v) Does anything need to be changed?

YEAR **1**

Sample 1

Area of Activity: Games.

Unit of Work: Introduction to throwing and catching a large ball.

Relevant National Curriculum PE Statement: pupils should be taught to explore, practise and develop a variety of ways of sending, (including throwing) receiving and travelling with a ball and other games equipment.

Learning Intentions: the children will learn to throw, catch, bounce and kick a large ball, individually and cooperatively with a partner. They will make up some activities of their own using large balls.

Development over six lessons

The children will continue to improve their running skills. They will work on their throwing and catching skills at their own level where possible. Each lesson will end with a quiet activity.

(i) Familiarization with a large ball.

Running activities to improve style.

Free experimentation with a large ball.

Children will learn to play 'Tadpole'.

(ii) Rolling and dribbling with the feet.

Running activities including how to stop suddenly.

Rolling a ball through each other's legs.

Kicking a ball through each other's legs.

Making up activities with a partner to include rolling and kicking.

Playing 'Tadpole'.

(iii) Throwing and catching on the spot.

Running activities to improve swerving and dodging.

Individually — throwing the ball up and catching it.

In pairs — rolling to a partner, kicking to a partner, throwing to a partner, introducing how to receive the ball.

In pairs — making up activities to include throwing and catching.

Playing 'Tadpole'.

(iv) Throwing and catching on the move.

Running activities to improve stamina.

Throwing and catching individually on the move.

Throwing to a partner so he has to move to catch.

Introducing different ways of throwing.

Playing 'Dodge Ball'.

(v) Bouncing.

Running to improve stamina.

Bouncing the ball — individually — bouncing on the spot and on the move, two-handed and one-handed.

Bouncing to a partner, the ball to bounce in a hoop.

Making up an activity based on bouncing the ball with a partner.

The children will teach their activities to other pairs for them to learn.

Evaluation with the children of the learned activities.

(vi) Consolidationp.

Running to improve stamina.

Free play with large balls working individually on rolling, kicking, throwing, catching and bouncing.

With a partner either making up activities or practising activities made up previously.

Playing 'Tadpole' and 'Dodge Ball'.

Criteria for the evaluation of this unit of work

(i)   Has the children's handling of a large ball improved?

(ii) Can they all bounce, throw, kick and catch a large ball?

(iii) Can they work cooperatively with a partner?

(iv) How successful have the games been?

(v)   Does anything need to be changed?

Sample 2

Area of Activity: Games.

Unit of Work: Improving basic skills.

Relevant National Curriculum PE Statement: pupils should be taught to develop and, practise a variety of ways of sending, (including throwing striking, rolling and bouncing) receiving and travelling with a ball and other games equipment.

Learning Intentions: by introducing a skills 'circuit' the children will have opportunity to practise their skills in different contexts, it is intended that the children will improve their coordination and they will also have opportunity to play a variety of games to increase their awareness of the nature of games played.

Development over six lessons

Each lesson will start with simple activities to improve coordination. A skills circuit will be set up and the children will rotate from one 'station' to the next. The lesson will end with a game and a calming down activity.

(i)   Running skills

The children will practise running, stopping, swerving and dodging.

A circuit will be set up and the activities explained to the children.

Station A: One child spins a hoop. The rest bounce large balls until the hoop has 'died', i.e. stopped spinning. They take it in turns to spin the hoop.

Station B: Each child has a quoit and a bean bag. He bowls the quoit along the ground and then tries to hit it by throwing his bean bag at it.

Station C: A large ball is balanced on a quoit. Each child has a bean bag. They throw their bean bags at the large ball, in turn, and try to knock the ball off the quoit.

Station D: Cones are placed in a line, one metre apart. At the end of the line a goal is made from two cones, side by side, one metre apart. The children, in turn, dribble a large ball, using the feet, in and out of the cones. They then try to score a goal by kicking the ball into the space between the two end cones.

Other stations can be added.

(ii) Football dribbling skills

The children practise dribbling a ball with the feet in and out of each other.

They rotate to a new station.

They learn to play 'Rainbow'.

(iii) Target skills

The children play 'Aunt Sally' i.e. in pairs, one child makes a 'mouth'. The other throws the bean bag into the mouth.

They rotate to the next station.

They end up by playing 'Rainbow'.

(iv) Skipping
The children practise skipping using skipping ropes.
They rotate to the next station.
They play 'Aunt Sally' and 'Rainbow'.

(v) Skipping continued
The children practise their skipping.
They have a quick turn at each station.
They learn to play 'Octopus'.

(vi) Consolidation
The children choose between skipping and football dribbling.
They practise bowling a hoop or a quoit.
They play 'Rainbow' and 'Octopus'.

Criteria for the evaluation of this unit of work

(i) Has the children's coordination improved?
(ii) Have their basic skills improved?
(iii) How successful were the circuit activities?
(iv) How successful have the games been?
(v) Does anything need to be changed?

YEAR 2

Sample 1
Area of Activity: Games.
Unit of Work: Bat and ball skills.
Relevant National Curriculum PE Statement:
pupils should be taught to develop and, practise a variety of sending (including throwing striking, rolling and bouncing) receiving and travelling with a ball and other games equipment.
Learning Intentions: The children will improve their running skills, they will learn to control a ball using a play bat, and will continue to play a range of games.
Development over six lessons
Some children will be more able to control a ball with a bat than others. Much of the work will be practising the skills to become more efficient at them. The children who are proficient will be given opportunity to progress on to more difficult tasks. Each lesson will end with a calming activity.

(i) Using the hand as a bat
The children will practise their running skills with emphasis on stopping suddenly. They will practise bouncing small balls with their hands and patting them up into the air.
They will make bouncing and patting patterns and teach them to each other.

(ii) Using the bat on the ground
The children will practise their running skills with emphasis on swerving and dodging.
They will work with a partner at sending the ball to each other along the ground using play bats, (sitting down facing each other if the ground is suitable).
The children will learn to play 'Crabs and Fishes'. Half the class are crabs and stand in hoops. The rest are fishes. On the ground are bean bags representing food. The fish try to collect the food, (one bean bag at a time) without being caught by a crab. If caught they become a crab and join the crab in the hoop.

(iii) Using the bat to pat bounce a ball
The children will practise running, trying to build up stamina
They will practise pat bouncing small balls using play bats.
They will pat bounce the ball to a partner who tries to pat bounce it back.
If this is too difficult for some, they can practise sending the ball along the ground.
The children will play 'Crabs and Fishes'.

(iv) Using the bat to pat a ball up into the air
The children will practise running to improve stamina.
They will practise patting small balls up into the air using play bats.
They will make up patterns based on patting the ball up and pat bouncing it.
They will teach each other their patterns and evaluate them.
They will play 'Crabs and Fishes'.

(v) Using the bat to pat a ball up into the air with a partner
The children will practise skipping to

improve stamina. They will practise patting small balls up into the air.

If this is too difficult for some they can practise the previous skills.

They can pat small balls to a partner to pat back after letting them bounce.

They will learn to play 'Tadpole'.

(vi) Consolidation

The children will practise skipping.

They will play with a partner using bats and balls, choosing their own activities.

The will play 'Crabs and Fishes' and 'Tadpole'.

Criteria for the evaluation of this unit of work

(i) Have the children's running ability and stamina whilst skipping improved?

(ii) Have they learnt to control a ball using a play bat?

(iii) Was it possible to extend the more able by giving them more challenging tasks?

(iv) Does anything need to be changed?

Sample 2

Area of Activity: Games.

Unit of Work: Making up games.

Learning Intentions: children will learn to plan, perform and evaluate their own games. Cooperation with a partner will be emphasized.

Development over six lessons

The children will be encouraged to write down the rules of the games they make up. These will be printed out on the class computer and laminated. They will then be made available for the children to use in other lessons and if possible at play times. The lessons will start with simple chasing games and end with quiet activity.

(i) Using a large ball

The children will play 'Tom and Gerry'.

They will be given one ball between two.

The task will be for 'A' to roll the ball between 'B's' legs and then make up a game developing this idea. The games must be given names.

The teacher will choose two or three good examples for the rest to try.

(ii) Using hoops and balls

The children will play 'Tom and Gerry'.

They will make up games in pairs using a hoop and a ball.

The ball has to bounce in the hoop.

The teacher will choose two or three examples for the rest to try.

(iii) Using quoits, balls and cones

The children will play 'Busy Bee'.

Working with a partner, each pair will have a quoit, ball and a cone.

They will make up a 'How Many?' game in which the quoit has to be thrown over the cone.

The teacher will choose two or three examples for the rest to try.

The children will evaluate the games they have played.

(iv) Choosing equipment

The children will play 'Busy Bee'.

In pairs, they will choose two pieces of equipment and make up a 'How Many?' game.

The teacher will choose two or three examples for the rest to try.

The children will evaluate the games they have played.

(v) Game-making in bigger groups

The children will play 'Catch My Tail'.

Those children who can manage to work in fours can make up a game using a large ball which has to be rolled along the ground.

The rest can choose a piece of equipment and either make up a game individually or with a partner.

The teacher will choose a good example of a game for four children for them all to try.

(vi) Consolidation

The children will play 'Busy Bee' and 'Catch My Tail'.

They will choose from all the games they have made up during the unit of work. This may have been done before the lesson starts.

They will end by playing 'Tom and Gerry'.

Criteria for the evaluation of this unit of work

(i)   Were the children able to make up their own games?
      Could they cooperate with a partner?

(ii) Were the rules of the games written down?

(iii) Were any of the games played at play-times?

(iv) Were the children able to evaluate the games they made up?

(v)   How successful have the taught games been?

(vi) Does anything need to be changed?

Chapter Four

Gymnastic Activities in the Early Years

Introduction

Why include gymnastic activity in the PE programme?

Gymnastics is a physical discipline in which the performer uses the body to demonstrate skill and daring in such a way that the movements are pleasing to look at. Every part of the body is involved in producing an aesthetic, stream-lined action, showing an acute awareness of the form, line and shape of the movement, together with an understanding of how to produce a series of actions that are fluent, smooth and exciting. This requires coordination, strength, suppleness and stamina, an ability to maintain balance both whilst still and moving, and knowledge of how to initiate turns on the ground and in the air.

There is sometimes confusion concerning the place and nature of gymnastics in the early years. On the television we see the highly skilful young gymnasts performing sequences on the floor, demonstrating amazing balancing feats on the bar and vaulting over a horse with ease. This is followed by the tense moments waiting for the judges' decisions and the medal awarding ceremony. Is this what we are aiming for?

On the other hand, schools sometimes put out a range of apparatus one day a week for each class in turn to climb on. It is often referred to as the 'large apparatus' lesson, or the 'climbing lesson'. Is this what gymnastic activity in an educational, i.e. learning context, is all about?

'Too often children are turned loose on various forms of equipment and expected magically to develop efficient forms of movement behaviour on their own. Only through wise guidance, thoughtful inter-action and careful planning can we assure the proper development of children's movement abilities.' (Gallaghue, 1982)

If we accept the concept that the learning process is to do with building on previous experience, as in principle 1 described in chapter 1, then our starting point is to look at what actions the children can already do when they start school. In fact they can roll, climb, crawl, walk, run, slide and jump. By the time they are 7 they can do all the basic actions.

Competitive gymnasts use these basic actions but develop them to a highly skilled degree.

We must also be aware of the nature of play and build on the ethos of the nursery school by providing situations in which learning can take place. These must be structured in such a way that ALL children can benefit, (see principle 6) having an opportunity to explore, select and practise the basic actions, in a way most beneficial to them.

All will agree that the body needs exercise. The more exercise the body gets up to the age of 6, the thicker the layer of cartilage in the joints becomes.

'If joints are subjected to suitable all-round stress during the formative years of child-hood, they will be well supplied with nourishment. This, in turn, leads to a thickening of cartilage, thereby providing better protection against the kind of injury caused by excessive stress. A joint which is not subjected to any kind of stress . . . reacts in an opposite manner; that is the cartilage thins out.' (Wirhead, 1984)

We must therefore provide opportunities for the children to strengthen their muscles, maintain flexibility in the joints and build up stamina, even more so today when children are not able to climb trees, jump off walls, and play unrestrained and unsupervised.

So in the infant school, gymnastics is about using the natural body actions as in competitive gymnastics, but in order to make the learning process meaningful for the children we use a range of strategies to help them develop both physically and in their understanding of what and how the body can move.

We do this by setting challenging open-ended tasks that the children can respond to at their own level. We create situations where the children can use their natural actions to climb up, go under, jump off pieces of apparatus. We make them aware of the surrounding space and how this can be used to advantage. We encourage them to make up their own phrases of simple movements linked together, which they can perform to the rest of the class if they choose to. 'Look at me!' is a frequent cry in the infant school.

When they are ready, we teach them specific skills, widening their range of movements. All the time we help the children to think about what they are doing and how they are performing, emphasizing the controlled and safe use of the body, without losing the daring and challenging aspects which play a part in gymnastic activity.

In order for this to happen we need to plan carefully, (see principle 2) moving the children on from the movement education in the nursery and preparing them for more stylised, skilled bodily action which has a clearer resemblance to recognised gymnastic forms in the later years. This we do by providing:

'. . . a "gymnastics" environment' in which children can progress at their own rate from moving instinctively and hesitantly to performing competently, with understanding and awareness.' (Manners and Carroll, 1991)

Curriculum content — areas of experience the children should have in gymnastic activities

Introducing the actions

The National Curriculum Physical Education Statutory Orders identified the basic actions in gymnastic activities as:

'. . . travelling using hands and feet, turning, rolling, jumping, balancing, swinging, and climbing.'

In games lessons the actions involved can be introduced gradually in a hierarchical way so that the children become more skilful, but at the same time the play element can be maintained. The children will be more familiar with games skills on arrival at school and most will have had an opportunity to throw, catch and kick a ball.

In gymnastics the whole approach is different, so we need to look at how these actions are developed in a different vein. Children will not be familiar with gymnastics as a recognized discipline and the actions involved will have previously been used very objectively.

In the first instance the children must learn to recognize actions that they have, in the past, performed instinctively without thinking about what they do.

To introduce this awareness we can apply the same approach used when learning language. In this instance the first words learnt are the names of objects, so in gymnastic activities we can help the children to learn the names of the actions involved.

In the reception class a unit of work can be

built up of naming the actions such as running, sliding, hopping, skipping, rocking and rolling.

Two or three actions are chosen for each lesson and the emphasis is put on getting the children to do the actions and to make the link between what they do instinctively and putting a name to what they do. For example in the first lesson we can practise ways of walking and running and stopping and then we can ask the children to 'walk' in and out of the apparatus, 'walk' up to the apparatus, climb on it and then 'walk' up to another piece of apparatus.

The next lesson could concentrate on naming spinning, sliding and pushing and pulling actions. These could be explored on the floor and then the children could 'find places to slide along on the apparatus'.

At the time the teacher is emphasizing the name of the action. She could choose a child to perform an action and then ask the children, 'what is the name of the action Peter is doing?'

In Year 1 the same actions are used but the emphasis is put on becoming more aware of the actions. For example, if the session is on spinning and sliding, then a range of ways of doing these actions is explored. Just as in language a child having learnt the word 'dog' will use it when he recognizes a dog in the street, and when he sees a picture of a dog in a book.

In Year 2 the actions are used for more specific purposes. For example, jumping may be used to get on to a piece of apparatus, over something or across a mat. The children are now ready to begin to link actions and make simple phrases fulfilling the National Curriculum Statutory Orders which say,

'Pupils should be taught to link a series of actions both on the floor and using apparatus, and how to repeat them.' (Key Stage 1: Gymnastic activities)

Introducing the children to use the space around them

Reception children are told as soon as they enter the hall to, 'find a space'. When you think about it we are asking the impossible. A space is intangible, once you have found it it has gone. They have found their PE bags, looked for their tee shirts, found a partner to walk with them down the corridor and now they are looking for a space!

If you ask them to stand on a spot on the floor away from all the other children, this can become a personalized place which we refer to as a 'magic' spot. Children become very adept at finding their 'magic' spot and it is an easy, quick way of spacing them out.

As with the actions, the children need first of all to become familiar with the space around them and how it can be used.

This can be done by getting them to go from one spot to another in different ways, taking up big spaces by using all the body and taking up little spaces by tucking up small, learning to stop suddenly in a space and making different shapes with the body in a space.

In Year 1 we can develop this by making the children more aware of the space by introducing concepts of 'high' and 'low', moving 'up to and away from' other children and apparatus and moving on 'wide and narrow' surfaces on the apparatus.

In Year 2 this could be developed by looking at ways the space can be used to travel in different directions.

Introducing the children to using specific parts of the body

In the reception class we can identify different parts of the body by naming them, for example, hands and feet, emphasizing how and where they can be put when moving on the floor and climbing on the apparatus, and we can introduce the children to identifying ways in which the weight can be taken on backs, tummies, knees and elbows.

In Year 1 we can put the emphasis on increased awareness of what the hands and feet can do and ways they can be used to support the body whilst travelling along. Travelling on backs, tummies, knees and elbows can be developed both on the floor and on the apparatus. The children also need to explore how these parts can be used to balance on whilst keeping still.

Using these parts of the body to take the weight of the body whilst still and whilst moving can form a unit of work in Year 2. The children need to discover how the weight can be transferred from one part to another in a rocking action, for example.

Introducing the children to specific skills

These include running, stopping, jumping and landing, rolling and cartwheeling.

> 'Pupils, plan and perform simple skills safely.' (National Curriculum PE End of Key Stage Description.)

Running and stopping: See 'running actions' in chapter 3.

Jumping and landing

> 'Children need to feel the strong thrust upwards through the legs and feet to get height. This can be increased with a vigorous upwards swing of the arms.' (Manners and Carroll, 1991)

On making contact with the floor the children MUST 'give' in the knees to absorb the impact.

At first the children should jump from both feet and land on both feet so that there is not too much strain on one leg and they remain symmetrical throughout and can therefore keep their balance. Whilst in the air they can make different shapes with their bodies, (wide, pin, tucked up) and they can learn to jump in different directions.

The children can experience the difference between landing and 'giving' into the floor, sometimes referred to as 'squashy' landings, and resilient bouncy jumps in which the landing is deflected by another jump upwards.

Combining a run and a jump is a skilled movement pattern and should not be introduced too early as it involves taking off from one foot instead of both.

Children can practise hopping and skipping, which is a hop on one foot followed by a hop on the other foot. Too much hopping on the same leg should be avoided.

All these jumps can be put into little patterns of movements which the children can make up for themselves. They can show these to other children, teach other children their patterns and maybe put two or more patterns together. Jumps can be linked with other movements to make patterns, such as rolling, jumping and balancing.

Apparatus can be used to help children jump onto and off something. They should learn to land safely in the middle of a mat on both feet with knees bent. Putting the hands down in front of them should be avoided if possible. They must not land on their knees.

Rolling

At first the children should experience the rolling action by going sideways, stretched out, 'like a log'. They can also roll sideways tucked up into a tight ball.

Forward rolls should not be taught before the age of 6 unless supervised by an adult on a one-to-one basis. This is because the bones and ligaments are not fully formed in the neck and permanent damage may result if the head is not fully tucked in.

Backward rolls are very difficult to coordinate and need to be taught when the child is really ready and not before.

Mats should be used for rolling actions to prevent the spine from bruising.

Rolling can be used in movement phrases, such as a tucked sideways roll followed by a stretched jump.

Cartwheels

These are the safest way to teach taking weight on the hands because the action is sideways thus diminishing the danger of falling forwards on to the face. Children can be taught mini-cartwheels, i.e. the wheeling action is mastered with bent legs. Then they can progress on to doing the action correctly.

The teaching process

At times the teacher will give the children a task to do which is very specific, such as, 'Jump up and down on the spot'. This may be to get the children warm, to introduce the focus of the lesson which may be on jumping actions, or to improve and develop a specific skill.

Much of the work will be of an exploratory nature giving the children an opportunity to respond individually. In this way they will work through the process of selecting, practising and perfecting their own actions. The task set will most likely begin with the words, 'Find a way of . . .'

Whilst the children are working, the teacher should circulate giving praise and encouragement. She should verbalize the responses to help the children recognize the names of the actions, and to acknowledge what the children are doing, for example she may say, 'Mary is sliding on her back'. She should make suggestions and maybe stand beside a child to give him confidence. Physically supporting children and holding them as they move should be kept to a minimum since they should be working within their own capabilities.

The children must work quietly and concentrate on what they are doing, although they will

need to talk on occasions. The teacher should stand where she can see the whole class.

After observing carefully how the children respond to a task, she needs to begin to formulate the next task. It might be that she stops the children and chooses a child to demonstrate to the others how he has chosen to move. This would be followed by a discussion on what he has done. The next task, then, could be for the other children to try to copy what they have

seen or incorporate the movement demonstrated in to their own movements in some way.

A simple task could then be developed, for example, 'Let's jump up and down on the spot' could become, 'Find ways of going along when you jump'. On the apparatus the task could be, 'Find places where you could jump' followed by, 'Find places where you could jump along'.

At all times the teacher should stress the quality of the actions, encouraging the children to perform as well as they can by stretching toes and fingers, landing softly and with control, jumping high, tucking up really small and so on.

Some of these points are developed in greater detail in chapter 1. 'Principles on which physical education between the ages of three and seven depend.'

General safety factors

The teacher will establish safety factors from the start. There will be a 'whole school' policy which everyone will follow, making it easier for everyone.

The LEA will have safety regulations which must be followed and the British Association of Advisers and Lecturers in Physical Education has produced a document, 'Safe Practice in Physical Education' (1990). This document identifies the following:

(i) Teachers need to be trained and qualified to teach safely — this may apply to secondary subject specialists (other than PE) teaching early years' children.

(ii) Apparatus needs to be checked regularly, and erected safely.

(iii) Children are taught the correct way of lifting and lowering heavy apparatus. (Bending the knees and keeping the back straight, gripping with the fingers and the thumbs uppermost all lifting together.)

(iv) Children are suitably dressed in clothing that will not catch on anything and allows for safe movement, whenever possible children should work in bare feet, long hair is tied back and no jewellery is worn. (Teachers should check their rings are not likely to scratch a child if they assist them in any way.)

What NOT to do.

Children should not jump off any piece of apparatus higher than themselves. Mats should be placed where children are likely to jump to cushion the landings, not placed indiscriminately in case children might fall — this is giving the wrong message; they need to know that they must move carefully in a controlled manner. For the same reason crash mats should not be used.

Children should not attempt forward rolls before the age of 6 unless supervised on a one-to-one basis. This is to prevent neck injuries. All rolling actions should take place on mats.

Moving objects such as balls and hoops (unless placed on the ground or fixed into activity skittles) must not be used in gymnastic lessons.

Apparatus must not be improvized, chairs and tables must not be used, stage blocks can be used if there is no likelihood of their slipping and there are no splinters or staples etc.

Games must not be played on the apparatus, nor should the apparatus be used in an imaginary way, i.e. as a jungle for the children to play on imitating animals. It should be used objectively.

Children should not be asked to make 'bridges' in which the back is overarched backwards. They may learn this in a gymnastics' club but even so should only perform such a movement after careful warming up exercises to flex the spine.

Children should not be asked to perform any movement that is outside their previous experience, i.e. a skilled, learned pattern, without careful description and build up. They should be able to do a movement without assistance (occasionally 'moral' support is all that is needed). Most of the time there will be an element of choice in what they do and where they do it both during floor work and work on the apparatus.

Mini-trampolines and springboards or Reuter boards should not be used as the children should learn to master their own 'natural' spring before going on to using artificial aids to flight.

Using large apparatus

Why use large apparatus in gymnastic activities?

Large apparatus provides:

(i) another dimension — an opportunity for children to see the 'world' from a different perspective;

(ii) opportunity to extend the range of movements a child can do on the floor;

(iii) situations for climbing, swinging, turning upside down, hanging, pulling, pushing, sliding, twisting, jumping on and off;

(iv) the need to make judgments concerning such things as distance, height, width, force, strength, etc.;

(v) challenge, requiring courage, thus increasing confidence, and an opportunity to test oneself and know one's capabilities resulting in a sense of achievement;

(vi) opportunity to strengthen muscles, particularly those of the arms and legs, maintain and improve the flexibility of the joints, improve endurance and stamina;

(vii) situations which require concentration, demanding perseverance and repeated practise, awareness of one's surroundings and other people, having to take turns and share, select and make decisions.

The aim of the large apparatus is therefore to provide a range of things for the children to use in order to make the work more challenging and exciting.

What apparatus will the children need to fulfil this aim?

They will need three or four nesting tables of different heights that have large surfaces on which the children can stand and feel safe. These can be linked up in different ways using planks, poles and ladders providing the tables have rungs on them. Agility tables serve a similar purpose but take up more storage space.

Benches are useful as they can be arranged in different ways, linked to other pieces of apparatus or used upside down.

A bar box provides a firm surface and the rungs can be used as hand holds. If it is in two layers it can be split for the younger children and used at its full height as a challenge for Year 2 children.

A climbing frame proves opportunity for children to challenge themselves and see the world from a different angle. One which has ropes attached are very popular and poles, ladders and planks can be fastened on to them at different heights.

Apparatus can be augmented by using hoops wedged in agility skittles, and quoits or carpet tiles with a non-slip backing, will provide 'stepping stones' for children to jump or hop from one to another, creating interesting pathways up to and away from the apparatus.

Plastic rods can be supported on cones for jumping over or sliding underneath.

Mats should be used to cushion landings from a jump and when rolling.

Setting out the apparatus

It is a mistake to have too much apparatus for the children as this can be bewildering, limits the floor space and restricts progression.

'Apparatus for the lesson, not a lesson for the apparatus.' (Rose, 1989)

The reception will need simple layouts of more individual pieces, fairly low, at different angles. They will need holes to climb through and wide surfaces to go along. The children are then free to choose where they go and will feel secure within that choice.

In Year 1 apparatus can be set up in more complex arrangements depending on the task in hand. Each arrangement is called a station. Children will be grouped and move from station to station every few minutes. They should be encouraged to approach the apparatus from different angles and create individual 'pathways' that go up to, along, off and away from it, thinking of the floor and mats as part of the apparatus. This will involve some 'turn taking' but discourages queuing and repetitive actions of one child following after another with no thought or choice in what he is doing. It also makes the best use of available space.

In Year 2 the apparatus will be set out in stations as in Year 1 but the children, grouped as before, will stay much longer at one station working on an action phrase which involves much more experimentation, selection and practise. They should be able to perform their phrase well and be able to evaluate that performance.

'Pupils should be taught to link a series of actions both on the floor and using apparatus, and how to repeat them.' (National Curriculum PE Key Stage 1)

The apparatus should be stored near where it is going to be used. The children can learn how to set it out if they are taught in simple stages. It saves time if the same children do the same task each lesson, for example, Peter and Mary attach the plank to the red nesting table as soon as Tom, Jane, Susan and George have set it in position. This does not necessarily mean they are going to be working on it. The same apparatus layout should last for a unit of work.

The children need to be taught how to lift correctly by bending their knees; they must know how many children are required to lift heavy things and never to lift anything over the heads of other children. They must not climb on anything until told to do so giving the teacher time to check that everything is secure. The teacher can stagger the setting out and putting away so that she can keep an eye on what is happening.

There are several ways of setting out the apparatus involving the children, and schools should devise a policy which the teachers follow. Reception children can learn to put out mats and small tables; Year 1 can learn to put out planks and benches; Year 2 can learn to put all the rest out.

The climbing frame should be one which all children can handle with supervision but some makes of climbing frame are very heavy and cumbersome, in which case these can be erected before the lesson providing they do not take up too much floor space.

When grouping the children to work on the apparatus it is worth remembering that two groups at a time can be accommodated on the climbing frame providing the children know which parts they can use.

There are several ways of organizing the storage of the apparatus and setting it out with the children. This is developed further in chapter 8, 'Implementing a whole school policy in physical education in the early years'.

How to get progression during a unit of work

It helps to think of a unit of work as a build-up over half a term or six weeks.

Progression at Key Stage 1 in gymnastics activities does not mean a hierarchical development from one skill to the next, each being more difficult than the last, but rather a deepening of understanding which will be reflected in the quality of their responses.

One aspect of movement will be identified in the title of the unit of work and this aspect explored in a variety of different ways increasing the children's knowledge and understanding as well as developing the range of movements, for example, a unit of work for a Year 2 class on 'Using parts of the body', will involve using different limbs and joints to balance on whilst still and whilst moving, an ability to transfer the weight from one part of the body to another, and using the legs to jump. In this way they will become more adventurous, skilful in managing their body weight, and aware of what the body can do and where it can go.

Progression can be achieved by exploring movements individually and then linking them to form action phrases. This will involve the children in decision making. They can choose the order of the actions to be performed, the way they are performed, and where they are to be performed. For example, a reception class working on 'positional language' may work on jumping off the apparatus and then combine

this with exploring different ways and finding different places where they can get on it.

Throughout the unit of work, emphasis should be put on the quality of the movements. All children can stretch their toes and fingers or tuck up really small. They can learn to control their actions by moving carefully and thoughtfully. This does not mean that we wrap them up in cotton wool, but challenging and exciting movements can still, and indeed must, be done in a controlled manner.

In some cases and in particular in Year 2, the children might be able to work with a partner towards the end of a unit of work, to produce an action phrase on the floor.

So at Key Stage 1, progression can be seen as a broadening out of the basic actions which the children can already do, as well as learning a few simple skills such as forward rolls. At the end of a unit of work the range and variety, together with knowledge, understanding and skill have increased and the children can perform with poise, good style and confidence.

> 'Children can develop their potential for exploration through natural movement if they are challenged and guided in a safe but stimulating environment.' (Heath *et al.*, 1994)

The planning process

This will take place at three levels. In the first instance the school will have an overall planning statement which will identify the needs of the children and how these needs will be met. The year group will then decide on the focus of each unit of work and the class teacher will plan the unit of work in detail.

Overall planning

The needs of the children have been established as:

> building up strength, flexibility and stamina; exploring, selecting and practising the basic

actions, both on the floor and on apparatus, responding in an individual way; acquiring specific skills; understanding how the surrounding space can be used beneficially; developing both physically and in the understanding of what and how the body can move in response to gymnastic-like challenges.

How these needs will be met will be outlined in each individual school's curriculum statement describing the amount of time to be allocated to gymnastic activity, and the resources available.

Year planning

If we use the basic actions as our starting point then our units of work could be built up over the three years by:

(a) *Naming the actions* in the reception class;
(b) *Identifying the actions* in Year 1;
(c) *Using the actions* in Year 2.

These tie in with the way children learn to master language. At first they learn the names of people, animals, toys, food and so on. They then make the connection between the name and the object, they recognize people, they will identify a dog whilst out on a walk, they quickly know the names of food they particularly like. They will discover they can use these names in different contexts, they will put them into phrases, and later build sentences once they understand the process.

At the same time, the children need to learn that movement takes place in space. Following the same principle, units of work could be:

(a) *Familiarization with the space* in the reception class;
(b) *Being aware of the space* in Year 1;
(c) *Using the space* in Year 2.

We have stated that, 'every part of the body is involved in producing an aesthetic, streamlined action' when a gymnast performs, so in the early years attention needs to be drawn to the part specific limbs and joints play in movement, so units of work based on this aspect could be:

(a) *Identifying parts of the body* in the reception class;
(b) *Being aware of parts of the body* in Year 1;
(c) *Using parts of the body* in Year 2.

Planning by the classteacher

Gymnastics' lessons need to be about half-an-hour in length in order for both the teacher input and the children's responses to take place in a structured way.

The structure can be kept simple and children need time to absorb and consolidate what they are being asked to do. To maintain a safe environment they should not be rushed or asked to move on from one piece of apparatus to another too quickly.

Warming up

As in a games' lesson, the children need to begin by getting familiar with the space, to listening to the teacher and getting warm. However, the emphasis in gymnastics is different from games and the warm-up activities need to concentrate more on how the actions are being done.

So the first task might be, 'run QUIETLY round the room', followed by 'jump SOFTLY up and down on the spot'.

Floor work

The main focus of the lesson is introduced and the children try out actions on the floor individually at first and then linking them to form simple action phrases. This gives them a firm and secure base on which to work.

Apparatus activities

Having explored a range of actions on the floor, the children can transfer these movements to different situations. This is done by providing apparatus of different heights, different widths, on a slope, something which swings, holes to climb through, planks to slide underneath and bars to hang upside down on.

This also gives the children a chance to strengthen the muscles in the legs and particularly the arms and shoulders.

Chosen movements can be tried out in different ways and the children given opportunity to select, refine and shape the movements with help from the teacher.

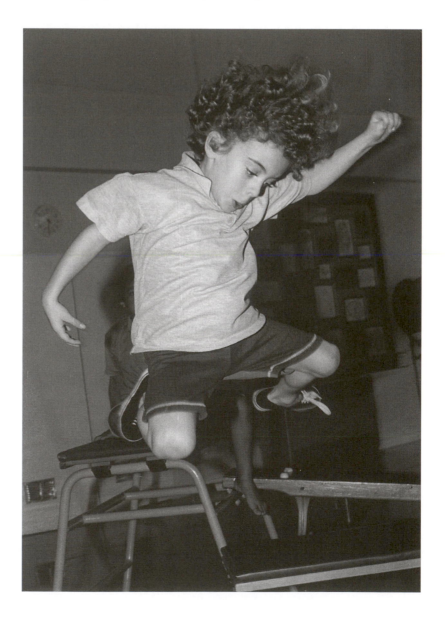

Calming activities

As in a games' lesson, once all the apparatus is put safely away, the children should be calmed down by doing an action very slowly or repeating an action from the floor work, concentrating on the quality of that action and then standing quietly.

Evaluating the success of the gymnastics programme

Teachers should keep in mind the end of Key Stage 1 Description in the National Curriculum, namely:

> 'Pupils plan and perform simple skills safely and show control in linking actions together. They improve their performance through practising their skills, working alone and with a partner. They talk about what they and others have done and are able to make simple judgements. They recognise and describe the changes that happen to their bodies during exercise.' (National Curriculum PE)

An example of a simple assessment procedure that can be used by teachers is included in chapter 8.

SAMPLE UNITS OF WORK FOR EACH AGE GROUP

RECEPTION CLASSES

Sample 1

Area of Activity: Gymnastic activities.
Unit of Work: Naming the actions.
Relevant National Curriculum PE Statement: Pupils should be taught different ways of performing the basic actions.
Learning Intentions: For the children to explore the actions of travelling and be able to name them. As this will be their first introduction to gymnastic activity since leaving the nursery, the main purpose of this unit of work is to lay down the 'ground rules'.

Development over six lessons: Simple pieces of apparatus will be placed in advance about the room providing opportunities for climbing, sliding, walking along and jumping off. Some apparatus will be very low and other pieces at a higher level for the more adventurous. Children will choose where they go and at what height they perform.

When they get back to the classroom after each lesson, they will draw a picture of themselves doing the actions and write the names (with help) of the actions underneath.

(i) Walking, running, and stopping
Children will walk in and out of the apparatus without touching it.
They will then run lightly in and out and stop on command.
They will walk and then put their hands on a piece of apparatus.
This will lead up to walking to a piece of apparatus and climbing on it.

(ii) Spinning, sliding and pushing and pulling
Children will learn to spin round and round on different parts of their bodies.
They will learn to push and pull themselves along on different parts by sliding.
They will find places on the apparatus where they can spin and slide.
They will watch one or two examples and name the actions they have seen.

(iii) Jumping and landing
The children will learn to jump and land safely on the floor.
They will make up 'jumpy' patterns.
They will find places on the apparatus where they can jump off safely.

(iv) Hopping and skipping
The children will learn to hop on one leg.
They will learn to skip.
They will choose ways of travelling and look at some examples.
They will name the examples, for example, sliding, hopping, spinning.
They will find ways of travelling on the apparatus.

(v)   Rocking and rolling
The children will explore ways of rocking from one part of the body to another.
They will learn to roll sideways across a mat.
They will find places on the apparatus where they can rock and where they can roll.
They will look at a few examples and name the actions.

(vi)   Travelling
The children will choose different ways of travelling on the floor.
They will name the actions they have chosen.
They will travel on the apparatus in different ways.
They will look at some examples and name the actions they have seen.

Criteria for the evaluation of this unit of work

(i)   Have the children understood the 'ground rules' and are they able to apply them?
(ii)   Can they name the actions they have used and seen other children using?
(iii)   Has the children's coordination improved when doing these actions?
(iv)   Was the apparatus layout appropriate?
(v)   Does anything need to be changed?

Sample 2

Area of Activity: Gymnastic activities.
Unit of work: Familiarization with the space.
Relevant National Curriculum PE Statement:
Pupils should be taught different ways of performing the basic actions of travelling.
Learning Intentions: For the children to use travelling actions to explore the surrounding space.
Development over six lessons: A similar arrangement of apparatus as that used in the previous unit of work, but with opportunities for the children to climb through hoops wedged into activity skittles at different angles, canes supported on cones for children to slide under and jump over, and non-slip carpet tiles. These will be placed around the bar box to act as stepping stones.
Some apparatus will be set out in advance and the children will learn to set out mats and benches.

(i)   Finding a space — magic spots
Children will stand on a spot, walk away from it and return to it.
This will be repeated doing different travelling actions.
The spot will be called a 'magic' spot.
Children will explore the apparatus.
Children will start on a magic spot, travel on the apparatus and return to the magic spot.

(ii)   Moving to a new space
Children will have two magic spots and travel in different ways from one to the other.
A few examples will be looked at for the children to name the ways of travelling.
Children will travel on the apparatus and look for new places to travel into.

(iii)   Stopping in a space
Children will run and stop in a space on a given signal.
Children will travel in different ways and stop in a space.
Children will explore the apparatus and stop in a space on it, and then carry on travelling. (In their own time).

(iv)   Big spaces
Children will walk in and out of the apparatus taking BIG steps.
It will be explained to them that BIG steps take up a lot of space.
Children will choose ways of travelling, taking up BIG spaces.
On the apparatus the children will travel, looking for BIG spaces.
The children will then make themselves BIG as they travel.

(v)   Small spaces
Children will walk in and out of each other as close as they can, taking up a SMALL space.

They will travel in different ways making themselves SMALL and taking up a little space.

They will travel on the apparatus looking for SMALL spaces to travel in.

They will then travel making themselves as small as possible.

(vi) Consolidation lesson

The children will try to find their two magic spots and find interesting ways to travel from one to the other.

They will travel from one to the other taking up BIG spaces.

They will slide from one to the other making themselves SMALL.

On the apparatus they will choose a magic spot, travel up to the apparatus taking up a lot of space, they will stop on the apparatus and then travel back to their magic spots making themselves SMALL.

Criteria for the evaluation of this unit of work

(i) Have the children become more fully aware of the space around them?

(ii) Can they move away from and back to a 'magic spot' in different ways?

(iii) Can they name the different ways of travelling they use and see other children using?

(iv) Was the apparatus layout appropriate?

(v) Does anything need to be changed?

YEAR 1 CLASSES

Sample 1

Area of Activity: Gymnastics activities.

Unit of Work: Being aware of different parts of the body whilst moving.

Relevant National Curriculum PE Statement: Pupils should be taught different ways of performing the basic actions.

Learning Intentions: Children will learn that different parts of the body can be used to support the weight of the body whilst travelling. They will work in small groups on the apparatus.

Development over six lessons: The climbing frame, benches, movement tables, box tops, and stools will form the main arrangement of apparatus, which the children by now can set up with help. Planks will be inclined onto stools to provide sloping surfaces.

The apparatus will be arranged in five stations and the children will rotate from station to station.

In the classroom the children will make cardboard models of themselves which they will cut out. The limbs will be joined at the joints by fasteners enabling the joints to move. They will label the parts of the body.

(i) Touching the floor with hands and feet

Children will explore different parts of the feet, for example, toes, heels, insteps and outsides.

Children will tap the floor with as many different parts of their hands as they can.

They will make up patterns based on tapping the floor with different parts of the hands and feet.

They will try to find places on the apparatus where they can tap the floor with their hands.

Starting on a magic spot, they will travel up to the apparatus using different parts of their feet, travel on it and jump back to their magic spots.

They will look at a demonstration by a child, and identify the different parts of the foot that have been used.

(ii) Touching the floor with different parts of the body

The children will tap the floor lightly with one elbow.

They will find other parts of the body to tap on the floor.

They will make up a 'tapping' pattern.

On the apparatus they will find places where they can have part of the body on the apparatus and part on the floor.

(iii) Travelling on hands and feet

They will recap on ways of travelling on feet.

They will find ways of travelling on hands and feet.

They will start on a magic spot, travel up to the apparatus on their feet, move on the apparatus on their hands and feet and walk on tip-toes back to their magic spot.

(iv) Travelling on hands and feet
The children will explore combinations of travelling on one hand and two feet, two feet and one hand, one foot and one hand.
They will make phrases of some of these actions.
They will explore the range of actions on the apparatus.
They will look at some examples and identify the actions being used.

(v) Travelling on backs, tummies, knees and elbows
The children will explore a range of sliding and spinning on different parts of the body.
They will try to travel on their knees and elbows.
They will make up phrases based on these actions.
They will try to move on these different parts on the apparatus.

(vi) Consolidation
The children will recap on use of parts of the foot and tapping the floor with different parts of the hand.
They will travel on hands and feet and various combinations of this.
They will travel on knees, elbow, backs and tummies.
They will make up a phrase using the floor and the apparatus based on a selection of these ways of travelling.
They will look at some examples and discuss the part played by the hands, feet, knees, tummies, backs, during the travelling actions.

Criteria for the evaluation of this unit of work

(i) Can the children identify the different parts of the body used by them and by other children when performing a travelling action?

(ii) Are the children imaginative in finding different parts of the body to travel on?

(iii) How good are they at making up phrases of movements?

(iv) Could they stay in their groups whilst working on the apparatus?

(v) Was the apparatus layout appropriate?

(vi) Does anything need to be changed?

Sample 2

Area of Activity: Gymnastics activities.

Unit of work: Stretching out and tucking up whilst moving and when still.

Relevant National Curriculum PE Statement: Pupils should be taught different ways of performing the basic actions.

Learning Intentions: The children will learn to feel what it is like to extend the body fully whilst moving and whilst still, and to tuck the body up as small as possible whilst moving and whilst still.

Development over six lessons: The children will work in six groups. They will be responsible for setting up their own group apparatus with help.

(i) Holding stretched and tucked positions
The children will choose different parts of their bodies to balance and be still on and stretch their arms, legs, heads, and backs as much as possible, away from the point of balance.
They will then choose other parts to be still on and tuck up as small as possible. They will find places on their apparatus where they can be balanced and still, in a stretched position and in a tucked position.
They will start on a magic spot and travel up to the apparatus, be still on it in either a stretched or tucked position and then travel back to their magic spots.
Some examples will be looked at and the children will identify the stretched and tucked position.

(ii) Moving in stretched and tucked up positions
The children will practise stretched and

tucked jumps and rolling sideways in stretched and tucked positions.

They will choose other ways of travelling whilst stretched and tucked.

They will make up phrases of movements going up to, on and away from the apparatus either stretched out or tucked up.

Some examples will be looked at for the children to identify how the task has been attempted.

(iii) Rolling in stretched and tucked position
Children will practise stretched and tucked jumps.

They will work on stretched and tucked rolls, going sideways.

They will continue to work on the same tasks as lesson 2 on the apparatus.

(iv) Travelling on hands and feet
Children will do bunny hops with the body tucked up.

They will practise stretched jumps.

They will make phrases of stretched jumps and tucked bunny hops.

They will find places where they can do bunny hops, up to the apparatus, on it or away from it.

They will incorporate stretched jumps, off the apparatus, on it or away from it.

(v) Travelling on hands and feet

Children will continue working on bunny hops.

They will learn to do crouch jumps.

They will try to remember the phrases they made up in lesson 4 and add rolling actions going sideways, to their phrases.

On the apparatus they will work on phrases involving going up to, on and away from it up in stretched or tucked positions.

They will look at selected examples and discuss how the task has been attempted.

(vi) Consolidation lesson

The children will try to improve their bunny hops, crouch jumps, rolls and jumps bringing out the stretched and tucked positions of the body.

They will work on their phrases of actions. They will choose one apparatus station and work on a phrase of actions.

They will look at selected examples and identify the actions and the body positions.

Criteria for the evaluation of this unit of work

(i) Do they understand the concept of stretching the body out and tucking the body up, both whilst balancing and keeping still, and whilst moving?

(ii) Can they jump and roll with the body stretched out and tucked up?

(iii) Can they do bunny hops?

(iv) Are they able to incorporate stretched and tucked positions into simple phrases of movement?

(v) Was the apparatus layout appropriate?

(vi) Does anything need to be changed?

YEAR 2 CLASSES

Sample 1

Area of Activity: Gymnastic activities.

Unit of work: Using the actions.

Relevant National Curriculum PE Statement: Pupils should be taught different ways of performing the basic actions, and to link a series of actions both on the floor and using apparatus, and how to repeat them.

Learning Intentions: Having learnt to name and identify the actions in the reception class and Year 1, they will now learn to use these actions in different ways. They will learn to do a forward roll.

Development over six lessons: On the apparatus the children will work in six small groups.

Each group will set out its apparatus. Each station will consist of a combination of apparatus; boxes and stools being linked by planks and ladders. Children will stay at one station per lesson, working on an individual phrase of movements. From time to time these phrases will be observed closely by the teacher to help assess the achievements of the children.

(i) Recap on the actions

Children will walk, run, skip and hop in and out of each other.

They will practise jumping and landing.

They will roll sideways tucked up and stretched out.

They will travel up to, on and away from the apparatus using these actions.

(ii) With rotation

The children will travel and turn on a signal from the teacher.

They will spin round and round on different parts of the body.

They will learn to do a forward roll on the mats.

They will find places on the apparatus where they can turn round and/or turn over.

They will start on a magic spot, jump up to the apparatus, find a way of turning on it and roll across a mat.

(iii) <u>To travel quickly or slowly with control</u>
The children will do fast, bouncy jumps around the room.
They will slide along slowly then spin round quickly.
On a mat, they will roll quickly or slowly.
On the apparatus they will use a range of actions to travel quickly or slowly.

(iv) <u>To travel quickly or slowly — continued</u>
The children will recap on the previous lesson.
They will make phrases of actions which they will perform quickly or slowly.
They will look at an example and describe how the actions have been used.
They will make up phrases of actions going up to, on and away from the apparatus. They will use these actions to travel quickly or slowly.

(v) <u>To travel using movements that require different degrees of strength</u>
They will practise jumping strongly up into the air, with controlled landings.
They will slide on different parts of the body using a strong push or pulling action.
They will run, skip and hop as lightly as they can.
They will make up a phrase of actions showing movements that require strength contrasting these with movements performed lightly.
On the apparatus they will try out pulling their bodies up and along using a lot of strength.

(vi) <u>To travel strongly or lightly — continued</u>
They will recap on the previous lesson.
They will work on strong jumping actions.
They will try 'press-ups' on the floor.
They will try to improve their running, skipping and hopping.
They will perfect their phrases of actions showing movements that require strength contrasted with those performed lightly.
Each child will make up a phrase using the apparatus travelling up to it, on it and away from it. They will use the actions to travel strongly or lightly.

Criteria for the evaluation of this unit of work

(i) Are the children able to set out the apparatus competently?

(ii) Do they understand what is required to make up a phrase of movements that can be remembered and repeated?

(iii) Do they know that actions can be performed in different ways, i.e. quickly or slowly, with strength or lightly?

(iv) Was the apparatus layout appropriate?

(v) Does anything need to be changed?

Sample 2
Area of Activity: Gymnastics activities.
Unit of work: Using parts of the body.
Relevant National Curriculum PE Statement: Pupils should be taught to link together a series of actions both on the floor and using apparatus, and how to repeat them.
Learning Intentions: Having learnt to name and identify parts of the body, the children will learn to use these in different ways. Emphasis will be put on the linking a series of actions which they can repeat.
Development over six lessons: The children will progress from working in groups to being able to choose where they work. More time will be given to work on the apparatus so they can link a series of actions which they can repeat. These phrases will be used to assess the achievements of the children.

(i) <u>Recap on parts of the body that can take weight whilst moving</u>
Use feet in different ways to walk along.
Use hands and feet in different ways to go along.
Travel on other parts of the body.
On the apparatus use feet and hands in as many ways as possible.
Use other parts to travel on.
Start away from the apparatus, travel up

to it, on it and away from it taking weight on as many different parts as possible. Repeat the phrase several times.

(ii) <u>To take weight whilst still</u>
Find ways of balancing on feet and hands, one foot and two hands etc.
Find other parts of the body to balance on. Remember to lift all the rest of the body away from the point of contact.
Balance on one part, tip off balance and go into a roll sideways.
On the apparatus find places to balance on different parts of the body.
Start away from the apparatus, travel up to it, balance on it, travel away from it trying to link one movement with the next.
Practise the phrases several times and try to remember them.

(iii) <u>To transfer weight from feet to hands</u>
Practise bunny hops. Try to do them one handed, using alternate hands, one footed.
Find ways of going from feet to hands and back to feet.
Using the apparatus travel up to it, on it and away from it transferring the weight from feet to hands where possible.
Practise the phrases several times and try to remember them.

(iv) <u>To turn cartwheels*</u>
Practise bunny hops and crouch jumps.
Try these actions with a turn.
Try transferring weight from one hand to the other as the feet are lifted.
Choose a child to demonstrate a cartwheel.
Children practise the cartwheel action without trying to straighten the legs.
Children practise the whole action transferring the weight from one hand to the other and then on to one foot followed by the other.
Work on the phrases started last lesson. Add a cartwheel if possible.

(v) <u>To turn cartwheels — continued</u>
Recap on the previous lesson.
Children work on cartwheels. Those who find it difficult practise bunny hops and crouch jumps.

Children work on phrases using the apparatus. These are practised several times. The children watch one or two examples and discuss how the parts of the body are used.

(vi) <u>Consolidation</u>
Children use different parts of the body to balance on.
They practise transferring the weight from one part to another in different ways.
They choose an action and try to perfect it, thinking about how the different parts of the body can be used.
They perfect their phrases using the apparatus.
They look at some examples and identify how the parts of the body are being used.

Criteria for the evaluation of this unit of work

(i) Are the children aware of how different parts of the body can be used to support the weight of the body whilst moving and whilst still?

(ii) Are they able to transfer their weight from one part of the body to another?

(iii) Can they manage a cartwheeling action?

(iv) Can they make up, remember and perform a series of actions with control and good style?

(v) Was the apparatus layout appropriate?

(vi) Does anything need to be changed?

* Learning to take the weight on the hands through a 'cartwheeling' action is safer than learning 'handstands' at this age. This is because the body is moving sideways as the weight goes onto the hands, whereas in a handstand, the weight goes forwards. If for any reason the arms are not able to take the body weight in a cartwheel the child will tumble safely onto his knees. If, however, the arms give way in a handstand, the child will fall onto his head and possibly bang his nose. Controlling a handstand is extremely difficult.

Movement Education Leading to Gymnastics 4–7: A Session-by-session Approach by Manners and Carroll, describes the teaching of gymnastic activities to Key Stage 1 in much greater depth and includes the teaching of specific skills such as running, jumping and landing, rolling, and cartwheels.

Chapter Five

Dance in the Early Years

Introduction

Why include dance in the PE Programme?

We have established that throughout life movement is used in a variety of ways. One could argue that movement is functional, that is, we use movement to walk to the shops, stretch to get something off a high shelf, bend to pick up something off the floor, run to catch a bus.

However, if we only use movement to serve an objective purpose, we would be like machines moving about as robots. 'Every picture tells a story' is a slogan we say in amusement when a friend limps in to the office on a Monday morning after a hectic weekend.

Our personal body language expresses our inner feelings whether we like it or not, and either voluntarily or unconsciously we convey moods, emotions, sensations and reactions. In the same way we learn to read this body language in other people. We think to ourselves, 'He looks pleased with himself', 'I wonder what's upset him?' and so on, using an unspoken language that is communicated through movements however slight which are symbolic and representative of how we feel and the way we see others.

When we run we use a basic running action that is the same for everyone. The leg muscles expand and contract, the knee and hip joints pivot and rotate in a mechanical, routine fashion. Yet our style of running is a unique performance, affected by our feelings at the time. The sense of urgency if running for a bus, chas-

ing after a toddler in a play-like way, jogging to keep fit, sprinting to hand over a baton in a relay race, all reveal a personal interpretation according to the purpose of the activity.

Throughout history, man has linked these two aspects of movement together, the inner feeling expressed through the functional movement having been exploited to serve a specific purpose. Ritual jumping and stamping has been performed in an attempt to evoke the gods into making it rain on the crops, war-like chanting and dancing rituals have aroused and intensified aggression before going to battle, slow sensuous caressing was used to arouse passion at Roman pagan feasts. Many of these rituals can still be seen today, the New Zealand 'All Blacks' at the start of a rugby match, whirling dervishes in parts of Egypt, teenage raves at all night discos.

This is not to say we are aiming to invoke a trance-like state in the early years! But we cannot deny that this symbolic, representational, expressive aspect of movement is part of our heritage and make up, and we owe it to our children to give them the opportunity to explore, develop and enhance movement as a means of communication and expression of inner feelings.

'The dance is the mother of the arts. Music and poetry exist in time; painting and architecture in space. But the dance lives at once in time and space. The creator and the thing created, the artist and the work are still one and the same thing. Rhythmical patterns of movement, the plastic sense of space, the vivid representation of a world seen and imagined — these things man creates in his own body in the dance.' (Sachs, 1937)

Dance therefore is a means of conveying moods, attitudes and responses by bodily movement, through being involved in an artistic and aesthetic experience. The imagination is aroused resulting in exciting activity in which the body is used in a dynamic, expressive way, involving phrasing, pattern, shaping and using the surrounding space. Dance is about the flow of 'statements' and the relationship between one movement and the next.

With young children, the movements stem from within rather than being imposed, developing a heightened kinaesthetic awareness. As they progress new movements can be introduced in order to widen their experience.

'The fact is that, with children, things are lived rather than thought and there is a reliance, early in a child's life, on movement experience.' (Vygotsky, 1962)

Dance requires versatility in the way the body can be used, together with strength, suppleness and stamina, as does gymnastics.

The difference between dance and gymnastics lies in the intention of the performer. In dance, movements are used to express and communicate the performer's inner feelings. In gymnastics the movements, which may be very similar, are used more objectively in response to a physical challenge.

Children have the opportunity when making dances to select, refine and shape the movements in order to achieve the best possible results. This process is an educational experience in itself. Children learn to observe and analyse each other's performance and later this can be transferred to appreciating highly technical dance forms seen on the professional stage.

Curriculum content — areas of experience the children should have in dance

Dance and dancing — different kinds of dance experiences we can give early years' children

On the one hand we want to help children to make up their own dances, involving them in the decision-making, selecting and improving their performance and at the same time helping them to gain knowledge about how to use movement, basic choreography, and evaluating dance performances both of their own and others' making.

In the past this kind of dance has been known as 'The art of movement', 'Creative dance', 'Expressive dance' and 'Dance in education'. For our purposes we will simply refer to 'dance making'.

Children also need the opportunity to learn the patterns, steps and routines of our traditional national dances such as maypole dancing, Morris dancing, and Scottish dancing, as well as dances from other countries. Many schools use the BBC radio lessons which develop stories and ideas through movement.

All these different forms have common factors and can be justified within the curriculum for their own reasons.

Dance is a good way to keep fit. It involves the whole body, increases the heart rate and by its nature is recreative and fun. Dance requires concentration, an ability to remember sequences and phrases of steps and other movements, it requires an awareness of other people and being able to respond to them in a sympathetic way.

Dance requires skill and coordination. If children are going to try to learn more about Indian dancing, for example, they will need to be able to make small gestures with the hands and step with the feet at the same time.

Dance is all about rhythm. Movements have a natural flow to them and this can be used to enhance the actions. Some parts of a phrase can be stressed more than others, and stillness can be very expressive. Many dances have a rhythm of their own as in a waltz or Irish jig. Infants will enjoy stamping patterns to depict the 'pitter patter' of the rain, or use the rhythm of words in a nursery rhyme to move to.

Patterns and formations require concentration but are fun and rewarding to do. Dance is about performance and a knowledge of how these patterns can be established helps to give dance a structure that can be recognized by an audience. Children need to understand that dance is a means of communication and in order for this to happen certain 'rules' need to be established.

Children can use props in their dances. Ribbons in maypole dances and sticks in Morris dances are a recognised part of our heritage. Clothing such as a variety of hats can be used to good advantage when making up dances, and masks help to create characters.

All children can dance. We need to cling on to this natural, innate desire to move expressively and spontaneously. If dance is taught sensitively and continuously throughout school then the children will not become self-conscious and embarrassed as they grow older. We need to give them confidence, a sense of security, a chance to contribute and succeed by involving them in the learning process, regardless of race, gender, culture, a disability or particular talent.

For clarification, the term *dance* is used as an art form in which the children are involved in the creative process, and *dancing* as a form of dance mainly performed socially as in country and national dancing.

'Physical Education in The National Curriculum' identifies three areas of experience the children should have in dance at Key Stage 1, namely:

'pupils should be taught:
(a) to develop control, coordination, balance, pose and elevation in basic the actions, of travelling, jumping, turning, gesture and stillness;
(b) to perform movements or patterns, including some from existing dance traditions.
(c) to explore moods and feelings and to develop their response to music through dances, by using rhythmic responses and contrasts of, speed, shape, direction and level.'

The teaching process

How to involve children in the creative process of making up their own dances

Ideas for dances

These fall into the following categories:

- Stories, poems, songs.
- The environment — seasons, growth, nature, the sea, volcanoes, rivers etc.
- Sounds and rhythms, music, percussion, words.
- Objects — balloons, feathers, shells, newspaper, machines, toys.
- Props — masks, chiffon scarves, tinsel, hats.
- Events — fireworks, celebrations, festivals.
- People — characters such as those in nursery rhymes, working actions.

In fact any idea can be used in dance-making provided there is movement potential in it. If the teacher cannot easily recognize what movements can be done to represent the idea then she is better exploring it in another medium, for example in art, drama or creative writing.

Selecting the appropriate movements

Having chosen an idea for a dance the teacher needs to select three or four key movements which symbolize the idea. This is important in order to make the actions dance-like rather than mimetic or drama-like. This means the whole body should be involved, feeling and expression conveyed, and the rhythm enhanced. In fact it helps to think of the actions as being exaggerated, larger than life, with the body extended to its limit, or tucked up as small as it can be. It is the quality of the movement and not the situation which makes it dance-like.

For example, jumping, flickering, twisting and turning might be the selected movements for a 'Fire Dance'. These would represent sparks, flames and smoke.

Once the teacher has discussed with the children how these movements might be performed, she will then work on each movement. In order to get a balance she may well decide to contrast a fast movement with a slow one, a jerky movement with a smooth one. To spend too long on one kind of movement is tiring and can cause tension in the body.

Over the five or six weeks in which the unit of work will be explored, these movements will be developed in a variety of ways. The children may suggest that the sparks are best represented by doing twisty, jerky jumps and clapping at the same time.

Perhaps the children could work on a pattern of jumps repeating a chosen rhythm.

Flickering movements could be done with different parts of the body. A series of quick shaking actions could be done with the fingers, arms, trunk, and feet. Children could make up a phrase such as fingers, fingers, fingers, trunk, foot, foot.

The twisting and turning actions are slow and change from low to high level.

Composing a class dance with the children

When the movements have been practised, they need to be ordered in some way. In the reception class it may be sufficient to say, 'We will do the jumpy movements like the sparks, and then the flickering movements like the flames and then the twisting and turning movements like the smoke and then we will gradually sink down to the floor like the fire going out.'

In Year 1 a formation could be introduced in which the children are in three concentric circles like a bonfire. Those on the outside start off doing jerky jumps around the edge of the circle and then those in the middle circle start their flickering movements gradually moving into spaces like the flames travelling from one place to another and then those in the middle start their twisting and turning actions like the smoke.

By Year 2 the children could work in threes and be given more freedom in their interpretation. They might decide to have one child doing the jumps, one flickering movements and one the twisting and turning actions, but agree on a linear formation. Or they could start away from each other and travel towards one another doing jerky jumps, then go round each other doing the flickering movements and then in a circle, facing the middle do the twisting and turning actions, before dying down. The groups could then perform their phrases in canon, like singing a round, one group starting and then another, like a fire building up in intensity.

The teacher might decide that the children should work individually composing a phrase based on jumping, flickering and twisting and

turning and then use these phrases to compose a class dance. One child could start, another follow on until they are all moving and then slow down at the end.

Formations that can be used in class dances

(i) Beginnings and ending

Children should learn from the beginning to 'hold' a position, they can be taught how to move and 'freeze', to make 'statues' and to 'go and stop'.

This can be done using a tambourine to which they can move when it is shaken and 'freeze' when it is banged. Moving to music and making a 'statue' when the music stops is another way of getting them used to being still on a signal.

This will lead them into making clear beginnings and endings although it is accepted that these do not necessarily have to be static positions and there are other ways that can be used, making an entrance for example.

(ii) Middles — the form the dance will take

Individual dances

The structure for a solo for this age group will be very basic. The child will decide on the order of the movements and the number of times each movement is performed, although the child will find it difficult to repeat his dance exactly and it may well change each time he performs it. A dance which holds the attention will have contrasts in strength, speed and levels, show clear phrasing and an individual rhythm. The end of one movement should become the beginning of the next to give the dance flow and continuity.

Partner dances

These can take the following form:

• Matching or mirroring each other's movements.

- Copying each other as in a follow-my-leader form.
- Contrasting movements.
- A 'question and answer' form.
- Using each other as obstacles to go over, under or round.
- Partners can start away from each other and move towards each other.
- They can pass each other and go round each other.
- They can go away from each other.
- They can start facing each other, back to back, beside, behind one another.
- One can start high and one low.
- One can move fast and one slowly.
- One can 'mould' the other like a sculptor making a statue.

Dances for three children

Most of the forms for partner dances can be adapted for three children.

In addition three children can form a circle facing inwards, or outwards, and move clockwise or anti-clockwise.

A circle can revolve and spin, it can shrink and expand.

The children can start away from the circle and move towards it and move away from it.

Three children can make a triangular formation.

Three children can make a line, one beside the other, or one behind the other. The line can get longer or shorter, one end can be higher than the other, and then it can change in a wave-like way.

The advantage of three children is that it creates a 'two and one situation'.

Two children can circle around one, one can move in and out of two.

One can go up whilst two go down, one can go forwards whilst two go backwards.

Class dances

In the early years, the children are not likely to be able to cope with a situation in which more than three children are dancing to-gether. However, in a class dance the teacher could plan the format and let the children decide on the movements within it, having given them three or four movements to choose from.

All the above formations can be adapted.

The dance could start with children dancing individually, they could then meet a partner and dance together. The children could then dance in threes and finally altogether, perhaps in a circle, finishing in the same positions as they started.

The class could be divided into two groups:

Half the class could hold a shape or position whilst the other half dance in and out of them.
Both groups could rotate in two circles.
One group could form a circle and the other group form a line.

Much of what has been described for partner formations could be adapted for the whole class, for example, the groups can move towards each other, go round each other and go away from each other, one group can move quickly and one slowly. Smaller groups of children in lines which could weave in and out of each other, without breaking up the lines, perhaps in a 'follow-my-leader' situation. The lines could then join up and form one big circle, or two or three circles, one inside the other. The circles could spin and then the children break away into a space and move individually.

These basic formations provide a framework. The teacher can use them as suggestions to the children, for example when the children are working with a partner, she may suggest to one pair, 'why not try starting back-to-back?' and to another, 'what would happen if one of you were to stretch up high and the other to get down low at this point in the dance?'

The framework can be used as a starting point by the teacher. For example she may say to the children, 'With a partner, start facing each other and mirror each other's actions.' The children could say the words:

I am me
Me I am
Am I me?
I think I am

as if looking at their reflections in a mirror.

The relationship of the movements to the music or other accompaniment

Choosing suitable music

This can be very time consuming and it is not always easy to find exactly what you want. The BBC 'Let's Move' programmes have an advantage here and sometimes the music and the movements on the tapes can be adapted to meet the needs of the class. A small but relevant repertoire is probably easier to refer to than a vast range of music.

Young children need short pieces of music that have decisive phrasing to them. It is a good idea to put the music chosen on to a cassette so that the start of the piece that is going to be used is found quickly and easily. If the music has a short introduction, the children will not wait unless taught to do so; as soon as they hear the music they will start to move.

Children like music with which they are familiar and TV themes are useful. Electronic music is often a good accompaniment for dance. A tape of several short pieces can be put together if necessary, rather than trying to find one piece that will suit changes of mood, speed, and phrases at exactly the right time.

Music can be played loudly or quietly, evoking different responses from the children, and it can be faded out to good effect. Music should not be stopped in the middle of a phrase.

Different ways of using music

It can provide the background to the dance, setting a mood or atmosphere but does not dictate the movements at all.

Music can suggest the kinds of movements that will be performed. For example, children will respond to fast, lively music by running, skipping, jumping, twirling etc.

It can provide structure to the format of a dance. Part of 'Heaven and Hell' by Vangelis is made up of four short phrases with a pause between each; this could be used by four different groups moving in turn and 'freezing' during the pauses.

The rhythm of the music can determine the movements, although children will find this difficult and prefer to move at their own pace. An obvious example would be a marching rhythm but children cannot easily count as they perform and may well need help from the teacher.

A list of suggested music will be found at the end of this chapter, but it must be remembered that music, like everything else goes out of date. Care must be taken not to infringe copyright regulations.

Using sounds to accompany movements

Children enjoy making sounds, but care should be taken to ensure that they do not detract from the quality of the movement. Also it is important that the sounds do not get out of hand!

Sounds help the phrasing of movements, especially since phrasing is very much like breathing; for example, a long breath in could be followed by four quick puffs out, the sounds being 'Ooooooooh, ah, ah, ah, ah'. The movements would be, starting from a low position, gradually growing up to a full stretch, and then shrinking down in a series of four jerky actions. The children would enjoy recording the sounds and then moving to them.

Using words to accompany movement

Again the rhythm of the words can accompany the movements and the children enjoy saying them as they move. For example, 'Snap, Crackle, Pop' could provide a lively rhythm for leaps, twirls and jumps. Almost any words can be used. Children might like to dance to their names, or to different food, for example 'Sausages and chips' suggests three steps and a jump.

Speaking whilst moving

Children can say the words of a poem or nursery rhyme as they move. It is a good idea to repeat each line several times so that they have a chance to coordinate the movements with the speaking.

Using body percussion to accompany movement

The obvious example is clapping, but it need not be the hands which clap.

The feet can be clapped together when sitting down, or one hand against an elbow for example.

Stamping provides a simple rhythm so does drumming the fingers on the floor.

Hands can rub against tummies to provide a rustling sound.

The tongue, like the fingers, can click and a finger in the mouth can make plopping sounds.

Using percussion instruments to accompany movements

Children will find it very difficult to play an instrument and dance at the same time, so it will mean choosing one or two children to play whilst the others move.

Drums, tambourines, triangles, castanets and chime bars can be used to advantage. Again it is a good idea to record the sounds for the children to use in later lessons.

For a class dance a variety of accompaniment could be used. A piece of music could introduce the dance, the children could then move individually making sounds as they move. A big bang on a drum would cause them to 'freeze', and then they could march in and out of each other to a regular beat, getting faster and faster and finishing with a big jump accompanied by a big bang on the drum. This could be adapted to a 'Humpty Dumpty' dance perhaps.

Music, sounds, poems, words and percussion can also be the stimulus, or starting point for a dance.

How to explore aspects of dancing with children

Country dancing

The term, 'country dancing' is vague and undefined, yet we recognize a country dance when we see it or hear the music. For our purposes we are referring to a style of dancing in England which goes back a long time, based on simple formations and steps such as skipping, and slip-stepping. However, the basic formations are universal and can be applied to national dances of Scotland, Wales and Ireland and imported dancing such as Morris dancing which is very popular today.

The purpose of teaching country dancing is to introduce children to these recognized forms used in traditional dances, and to master the simple steps. The teacher can make up dances for her children as well as involving the children in making up their own dances using these formations and steps.

Dancing is a good aerobic activity and its inclusion in a physical education programme can be justified on health and fitness terms.

The social aspect of country dancing has its value and dancing together helps the children with a sense of identity.

The music, by nature, is lively, simple, tuneful and repetitive, which the children enjoy. Dancing is FUN.

With so much to cram into a physical education programme, it may mean that country dancing is just one unit of work for Year 2 children, or it could be used to replace outdoor games lessons when the weather is bad. It could be part of a health and fitness programme possibly tied in to a topic on 'Our Bodies' or 'Ourselves' the teacher stressing the aerobic fitness aspect, asking the children such questions as, 'Why do we get hot when we do these dances?' and, 'What happens to our bodies when we do these energetic dances?'

The following ideas are intended to help teachers select material for their children as and when appropriate. They do not form part of a detailed structured development plan in the same way as other specific activities.

Introducing children to different country dancing formations

Where partners are needed it is not necessary to pair boys off with girls. It may be that there is not an equal number of boys to girls and this can present problems. Children can choose their partners and other names substituted. For example they could be monkeys and bears, reds and blues, cups and saucers etc. It may help in some instances to use team bands to differentiate one from another.

Country dancing is about steps and formations. Children may find it difficult to do both so to start with they should have plenty of practise at doing one without the other.

Counting

When counting out steps for the children the teacher should allow for changes either in direction or steps, for example, 'one, two, three, four, five, six, seven, stop', or, 'one, two, three, turn', or 'forward, two, three, four, five, six, and stop'.

Accents should be placed on the first count each time and on the last count when it comes to the end of the dance.

Most dances for this age group will be built around the common time of four beats to a bar and four bars to a phrase. This can be used in one phrase of sixteen counts, or two phrases of eight counts. Probably the children will not be able to cope with too many changes coming too fast, so four phrases of four counts would be too difficult. Clapping to a rhythm will help. A tambour or drum can be substituted to save the teacher's voice and provide a contrast for the children.

Steps

Dances can be made up involving step patterns which the children do anywhere in the room. For example:

(i) walk anywhere and when I tell you, change to skipping;

(ii) now walk eight steps then skip eight times;

(iii) let's do this to the music (use a simple marching tune);

(iv) this time I want you to walk eight steps, skip eight times then clap for two lots of eight counts;

(v) now you choose when to walk, skip and clap. Remember there are two lots of clapping;

(vi) find a partner and choose one pattern and do it side by side. Then choose the other pattern. Can you put both patterns together and do one after the other?

(vii) now, instead of doing the patterns side by side find a different way of doing it, for example, towards each other, starting back to back, or going round each other.

This can be repeated introducing the 'slip step'.

The 'slip step' is stepping to one side, joining the other foot close to the first foot and stepping on it.

Galloping, although not used in country

dances is a fast, easy step, and can replace skipping if the children find this difficult. One step is longer than the other. The child steps forward onto one foot and then the next step is a short, quick one, placing the second foot in front of the first one so the timing is, 'tum-ti-tum'.

Formations

These dances can be performed to any march tune or country dance music with a common rhythm, i.e. four beats to the bar and four bars to a phrase.

(i)   The circle
      This is the simplest formation, and the oldest, going back to prehistory.
      Children can skip round freely, or holding hands.
      Reception children can do 'Here we go round the mulberry bush' type action songs in the first instance.
      Having gone round in a circle, the children can learn to go in to the middle and back again.
      A simple dance could be:

      'Rosie's Walk'
      skip round for sixteen counts;
      walk in to the middle for eight counts;
      walk out for eight counts.

      This could be developed into:

      'Around the Houses'
      skip round anti-clockwise for eight counts;
      skip round clockwise for eight counts;
      walk into the middle for four counts;
      walk out for four counts;
      stand still and clap for eight counts.

(ii) Two parallel lines. (A longways set)
      Children stand side by side with a partner. Identify the top and bottom couples.

```
top couple
  x    x
  x    x
  x    x
  x    x
bottom couple
```

The number of pairs should not exceed eight. A simple dance could be:

'The Railway Children'
Those in the left hand line follow the top child who turns to the right and leads the children around the other line and back to their places, skipping, for eight counts (casting off). This is repeated by the right hand line, for eight counts. Both lines then go simultaneously for eight counts. The top couple turn away from each other and meet at the bottom. They then come up to the top together, followed by the rest. They then stand still and clap for eight counts.

This could be developed by the top couple skipping down to the bottom between the lines whilst the rest are clapping so that when the dance is repeated there are new leaders.

(iii) Two lines facing each other

```
xxxxxxxx

xxxxxxxx
```

Children stand side-by-side in a line facing a partner. The lines can go forwards to meet each other, backwards away from each other, and change places. This is done by one line holding hands to form 'arches' as they approach the other line, those in the other line drop hands and go under the arches.
      A simple dance could be:

'Underneath the Arches.'

Both lines walk forwards towards each other for three counts and nod their heads on the fourth count acknowledging the other line.

They then walk backwards to their places for three counts and stamp on the fourth count.

They then walk forwards as before and change places by one line forming arches for eight counts.

The top couple hold hands and skip to the bottom for eight counts.

All stamp and clap on the spot for eight counts.

(iv) Four couples standing in a square. (A square set)

Eight children stand in a square. Two stand side by side at the top, two at the bottom, two on the left and two on the right, as follows:

```
        xx          (top couple)


   x              x
   x              x

        xx          (bottom couple)
```

The eight children can hold hands and move round in a circle, they can go into the centre and back again.

Each couple can, in turn, skip around the outside of the set and back to their places or the top and bottom couples can go at the same time, followed by the side couples.

The top and bottom couples can change places, followed by the side couples.

The top and left hand couple can do a 'right hand star' followed by a 'left hand star' followed by the bottom and right hand couple. To do this the four children put their right hands on top of each others' at head height to form a star, and skip round clockwise for eight counts, they then drop their hands, do a half turn to

the right and put their left hands on top of each other and skip round anti-clockwise for eight counts, ending up in their square formation.

A simple dance could be:

'Off to the Market'

Hold hands in a circle and slip-step anti-clockwise for sixteen counts, ending in the square formation.

Top and bottom couples skip round the outside of the set and back to their places for eight counts.

Side couples skip round the top and bottom couples for eight counts.

Top and left hand couples skip round in a right hand star for eight counts and then a left hand star for eight counts.

Bottom and right hand couples repeat the right hand star and the left hand star.

Helping the children to make up their own country dances

Once the children have learnt the steps and are familiar with some of the formations, they can make up their own dances. These will involve selecting, practising and perfecting the dances and every dance made up should be given a name. Children should have the opportunity to perform their dances either to the class or to another child. The dances made up could be collated into a class book of dances and put on display, or used by other children in other classes.

Initially they can dance on their own making up a sequence of two movements which they can do in any order, for example, stamping and skipping. This can be increased to four movements such as stamping, skipping, clapping and side-stepping. They will need help with counting and remembering how many steps they do, but this is not too important at first.

This can be developed to dancing with a partner and introducing a simple formation.

Children could progress onto making up dances in fours but the more children in a group, the harder it becomes to decide on what to do.

Children may like to include other movements and not conform just to the accepted step patterns. There is no reason why they should not do this. For example, spinning and twirling, hopping, different kinds of jumps, hand gestures etc.

Music

Any march tune is suitable, but remember unless it is specifically written for dancing, it will probably have an extra two bars between the 'A' tune and the 'B' tune and when the dance is finished there may be some music left over. This can be overcome by telling the children to wait for eight counts at the appropriate moment.

Most music written for country dancing, barn dancing, and Morris dancing, can be used for adapted dances, and many Scottish dance tunes appeal to the children.

BBC theme music is familiar to the children, the *Blue Peter* theme for example, and *Match of the Day*.

Many popular children's songs which are recorded on cassette can be danced to, such as, *The Sun has Got his Hat On* and *The Teddy Bears' Picnic*.

Nursery rhymes such as, *Baa Baa Black Sheep* are excellent to skip to.

Exploring aspects of a variety of dance from different times and cultures

There are several sources a teacher can go to in order to find suitable material and ideas for dances of different times and cultures.

Books are an obvious resource and libraries will be helpful.

There may be local clubs or people within the community who would be pleased to help, and ballet schools often teach national dances to their pupils.

Parents with different cultural backgrounds might like to share their dancing styles with the children.

Associations such as 'Cecil Sharp House' in London and the Physical Education Association will be able to provide information.

Local education authorities and local Arts councils often have dance officers who could be contacted, and possibly nearby secondary schools will have a dance specialist on the staff who could either provide help or know where to turn to to get assistance.

Most of the dances will be too complicated for early years' children so the teacher will have to identify the main characteristics and concentrate on these.

For example, a form of Indian dance tells a story through hand gestures whilst walking to a four-beat rhythm. Children could choose a piece of a story, such as Jack climbing a beanstalk, which they mime with their hands whilst walking along. This could be performed to a piece of Indian music.

In the same way, an Austrian dance by the children could consist of a modified 'Schuplatter', i.e. slapping the thighs, high kicks and clapping performed to a piece of yodelling music.

The planning process

Points to bear in mind when planning

In dance lessons, the process is as important as the product, the doing being as important as the end performance. But when planning a series of lessons, the teacher needs to know what form the end product will take so that she can work towards it, although she will need to have a degree of flexibility built in to cater for the responses of the children. This means the planning is more a series of pointers or signposts suggesting the direction the lessons will take, rather than highlighting specific areas of learning as in games and gymnastic activities.

Planning will take place at three levels. In the first instance the school will have an overall planning statement which will identify the needs of the children and how these needs will be met. The year group will then decide on the focus of each unit of work and the class teacher will plan the unit of work in detail around an idea or stimulus and an end product, i.e. a class dance.

Overall planning

Through dance-making the needs of the children will be met by involving them in the creative process of planning, performing and evaluating dance using their bodies as a medium for expression. The need to explore a range of feelings and emotions through movement fulfils the innate desire of the child to communicate with the world about him.

Year planning

The easiest way to meet the needs of the children is to use Laban's analysis of movement to identify units of work to suit the age group namely:

WHAT the body is doing —
what action? (jumping, stepping, sliding, spiralling etc);
focussing on what part? (hands, feet, backs etc);
what shape is the body making? (tucked up, stretched wide, elongated, twisted.)

HOW the body is moving —
quickly or slowly;
with strength and tension or lightly and relaxed paying attention to the rhythm and flow of the movement either individually or a common rhythm.

WHERE the body is going —
direction — rising up or sinking down forwards, backwards or sideways around the body, near to and far away;
level — high in the air or low near the ground;
pathway — straight lines, curves, zig-zags.
(Adapted from Laban, 1947)

Added to this are the relationships of one dancer to another, one movement to another in movement phrases, and the relationship to the music or other accompaniment.

Using this model the year group teachers may identify units of work for each age group. This will help to ensure progression from year to year. Where mixed age groups exist it may be necessary to work to a two-year plan as in other curriculum areas. As most tasks differentiate by outcome, i.e. the children respond according to their level of understanding rather than trying to perform a specific skill; this should not present too much of a problem in dance since many of the tasks will be open-ended.

For example, reception teachers may choose units of work focussing on the body actions, parts of the body, and shapes the body can make whilst moving. (*What* the body is doing.)

Year 1 teachers could focus on moving quickly and slowly, lightly and strongly, and moving to common rhythms. (*How* the body is moving.)

Year 2 teachers could concentrate on moving in different directions, on different levels and along different pathways. (*Where* the body is going.)

Although one aspect is focussed this does not mean the others are not included. For example, a jumping action is bound to include going up into the air, but for the purpose of the planning it is the action (i.e. what the body is doing) which is emphasized rather than the spatial aspect (i.e. where the body is going).

Planning by the class teacher

Having identified the main movement focus the teacher will decide on a stimulus or idea around which the lessons will revolve. This can be related to a topic, for example, a 'spider' dance could fit in with the topic of 'Mini Beasts'. If it were a reception class, the teacher could select ways of moving on the hands and feet in a crawling action to represent the spiders and running in straight lines with sharp turns to represent flies. A spider's web could be constructed from wool which the children could hold up at different levels and angles like a web, for the 'flies' to be trapped in.

Once the movements to be worked on have been established, the teacher then needs to plan the class dance, i.e. the end product, and how she will achieve this bearing in mind the fact that she needs to involve the children in dance making in some way.

Lesson structure

The lesson should begin with a simple warming up activity which will get the children used to the big space, physically warm, and mentally tuned in to listening and following instructions.

These activities should enable the children to respond in a fairly unstructured way, but at the same time the emphasis should be on the quality of the movements so that they are expressive in nature, for example, 'Choose a way of moving lightly to this piece of music.'

The development of the lesson is built around the selected movements which go to form the unit of work. Movement ideas can be explored, practised and perfected in a range of different ways.

These ideas provide the material for the class dance, which can be composed lesson by lesson until completed in the last lesson, or stored up until the time when the class dance is to be put together and performed. Either way, the class dance provides an end 'product', whilst the development is the process by which the dance is arrived at.

Each lesson should end with a calming down activity which brings the children together, particularly if they have been working in small groups, requiring a great deal of discussion. Activities should be slow, quiet and controlled.

If the theme of the lesson is cross-curricular, then work may be carried over into the classroom. Vocabulary explored through dance might be used in a different context such as poetry, creative writing or a story. There are often close links with art and design which could be explored. The theme of 'patterns', for example, would lend itself to being treated in this way.

Evaluating the success of the dance programme

This is difficult to do since the emphasis is on the qualitative aspect of movement and therefore not measurable in concrete terms.

The teacher should try to observe the involvement of the children in the activities, whether the whole body is absorbed in the action, or whether they are just going 'through the motions'. This includes watching the children's eyes; if they are looking at other children or out of the window then they are not fully involved.

She should try to assess the contributions the children themselves make to the dance-making process, how appropriate they are, how willing the children are to use and adapt them, whether they can remember them.

Above all her own enthusiasm for the lessons will be a guide to their success. If she is looking forward to developing the children's ideas then this is a good indicator. However, not all ideas and lessons fire the children's imagination and sometimes things can go wrong. If she can identify the problem and put it right all well and good, but if not, it may be better to scrap the idea and start again.

Dance is perhaps the only physical activity which does not necessarily depend on resources other than the body. Games lessons will most likely succeed, in the short term, if the children are given balls or other equipment to play with, gymnastics apparatus provides opportunity for the children to climb and keep active that way, the water in swimming provides a challenge to the children. Therefore dance lessons are more difficult to plan, requiring an ability on the part of the teacher to motivate the children, draw certain responses from them and then use these responses in a constructive way.

However these strategies are no different from those used in good classroom practice and if teachers can recognize the parallel between the process applied in academic work and in practical work of this nature, then she can teach dance successfully and competently.

An example of a simple assessment procedure that can be used by teachers is included in chapter 7.

SAMPLE UNITS OF WORK FOR EACH AGE GROUP

RECEPTION CLASSES

Sample 1
Area of Activity: Dance.
Unit of Work: Emphasis on using different parts of the body in a simple dance form.
Title of Dance: Rain, Rain Go Away.
Learning Intentions: To explore finger patterns, stamping and jumping rhythms, building on work introduced in the nursery.
Music required: 'Dance of the Little Fairies' by Sky.
Development of Dance idea over five weeks
Select from the following ideas and practise and develop over the five weeks:

(i) Practise all sorts of hand movements, for example, shaking, 'playing the piano', waving goodbye, clapping, 'pat a cake', clicking fingers, moving hands around the body, close to the body and away from the body, sitting on the fingers, stretching the fingers out etc.
Teacher does clapping rhythms for the children to copy.

(ii) Using lively music, (for example, Herb Alpert's 'Tijuana Brass') practise different ways of travelling on the feet, for example, running, skipping, hopping, walking on tip-toes, trotting etc.

(iii) Dance to the music, sometimes doing a hand dance and sometimes doing a foot dance. Can you dance with your feet and hands at the same time?

(iv) Practise taking big steps lifting the knees. Step to a rhythm, such as, step, step, step, step, run . . . and stop, repeat several times. Stamp to a rhythm, such as, stamp, stamp, stamp, stamp, skip, skip, skip. Make up a pattern including big steps, stamping and skipping.

(v) Practise big jumps, landing with knees bent low near the floor. Do a jumpy pattern around the room.

Class dance to be performed in week 6

(i) Children start on their knees. Drum fingers on floor to make it sound as if it is raining. Do this in a rhythm, i.e. drum . . . and stop, drum . . . and stop.

(ii) Stand and stamp feet on the floor saying, 'Pitter patter, pitter, patter' several times. Children stamp to the rhythm of the words.

(iii) Reach up and shake fingers. Gradually let fingers fall to the ground to represent the rain falling. Do this several times.

(iv) To music, take big steps as if wearing large wellies, then run and jump as if splashing in big puddles.

(v) Skip or jump chanting, 'rain, rain, go away, come again another day'. Do this several times. On the last time do a big jump on the final word, 'AWAY' and finish low near the floor.

Criteria for the evaluation of this unit of work

(i) Have the children understood the significance of choosing movements to represent the rain falling and splashing in puddles?

(ii) Has the awareness of what the feet and hands can do as a medium for expression improved?

(iii) Are they able to move to a simple, common rhythm?

(iv) Does anything need to be changed?

Sample 2

Area of Activity: Dance.

Unit of Work: Travelling Actions.

Title of Dance: *My Toys Have Come Alive*!

Learning Intentions: To discover that travelling actions can be performed in different ways.

Music Required: 'Belfast Hornpipe' played by James Galway.

Development of Dance over five weeks

Select from the following ideas. Try to get a balance in the lessons. do not spend a whole lesson on 'floppy' movements for example:

(i)   Practise marching about the room, swinging the arms and keeping the legs straight. Try keeping in step with a partner. Add turning and saluting — like a soldier.

(ii)   Have a look at some floppy dolls. Try to be floppy like them. Keeping your legs straight, walk upright then flop over from the waist letting your arms go floppy. Try turning and 'staggering' as you walk and flop. Practise falling over and sticking your feet up in the air. Get up by leaning on your hands and stand without bending your legs.

(iii)   Look at some 'action man' dolls. Make up some movements, for example, run, lie down, fire a gun. Crawl on your stomach, throw a grenade, duck your head.

(iv)   Practise moving one bit of your body at a time (puppets) in a series of jerky actions, pretend someone is pulling a string which makes the elbows move. Repeat moving hands, head, knees, feet etc. Fall over and get up with the strings all tangled up. Shake and untangle the strings. How does a puppet run, jump, skip, and hop?

(v)   Look at other toys and discuss ways of portraying the toys through movement. Play some lively music and let the children try out ideas of their own. Suggestions — spinning tops, robots, mechanical toys.

Class Dance to be performed in week 6

(i)   Children start in held positions — each position portraying a toy. When the music starts they all travel about the room in character.

(ii)   One group represents the toy soldiers. They march up and down the room whilst the rest 'freeze'.

(iii)   Another group then does a 'floppy' dance portraying rag dolls.

(iv)   A third group then does an 'action man' dance.

(v)   A fourth group does a 'puppet' dance.

(vi)   They all dance at the same time. When the music stops they 'freeze'.

Criteria for the evaluation of this unit of work

(i)   Have they learnt that travelling actions can be performed in different ways?

(ii)   Were they able to perform the class dance without too much help?

(iii)   Did they come up with some good ideas of their own?

(iv)   Was the music suitable?

(v)   Does anything need to be changed?

YEAR ONE CLASSES

Sample 1

Area of Activity: Dance.

Unit of Work: Moving at different speeds.

Title of Dance: *BRR. . . . IT'S COLD*!

Learning Intentions: To explore contrasts in speed through swirling, melting, freezing and tucking up.

Music required: 'Snowflakes are Falling' performed by Tomita.

Development of Dance idea over six weeks

Select from the following ideas, practise and develop over the six weeks.

(i)   Children practise running, leaping, spinning, swirling, turning over, settling etc. to represent the snow falling. Discuss with the children which movements can be performed quickly and which need to be done slowly.

(ii)   Practise 'freezing' — one part of the body at a time, for example, twist fingers, turn the head, twist the back, twist each leg in turn.

(iii) Practise lying on the floor relaxing. The teacher tries to get children to go 'floppy' by taking hold of an arm or leg and shaking it gently. Combine fast 'freezing' with slow melting into complete relaxation.

(iv) Find ways of tucking up small and stretching out wide, quickly, slowing, with a turn, on different parts of the body, in small groups.

(v) Pretend you are playing in the snow, making footprints, throwing snowballs, ski-ing etc. Some times move fast and sometimes very slowly.

Class dance

(i) To the music — children run, leap, spin, twirl, turn over, settle etc. to represent the snow falling. Emphasis is on moving lightly, sometimes fast and sometimes slowly.

(ii) Jack Frost (a child or the teacher) goes to each child in turn, shaking castanets, he 'freezes' by making a twisted shape, and staying still.

(iii) The sun (a child or the teacher) goes to each child in turn and gently beats a gong or cymbal and the child 'melts', i.e. he relaxes and slowly falls to the floor.

(iv) To music — children tuck up small and gradually grow up and open out wide, with a turn, on different parts of the body, or in a group, to represent bulbs and spring flowers opening out.

(v) To the music — children perform a lively, happy dance to represent the new born lambs gambolling.

Criteria for the evaluation of this unit of work

(i) Have the children fully explored the contrasts of speed that actions can be performed?

(ii) Were they able to perform the class dance without too much help?

(iii) Is their understanding of dance as an activity increasing?

(iv) Were they able to provide good ideas of their own?

(v) Does anything need to be changed?

Sample 2

Area of Activity: Dance.

Unit of Work: Contrast in light and strong movements.

Title of Dance: Balloon Dance

Learning Intentions: To help the children feel the difference between moving with strength and moving lightly.

Music required: Parts of 'Pictures at an Exhibition' created by Tomita.

Development of Dance over six weeks

Select from the following ideas. Try to get a balance between the strong and light movements in each lesson. Let the children watch you blowing up a balloon using all your strength to get the air into it. Discuss with them what will happen when you let go, and why it 'flies' like it does.

(i) Children lie on the floor, they gradually grow bigger and bigger as the teacher counts up to five. They do this with as much tension in the body as they can. They then get smaller in five counts.

(ii) This is repeated in different ways. The children can explore growing bigger in a series of quick jerks and smaller in one long 'sigh'. Tell the children it is like breathing in different ways. Let them make up different 'breathing' patterns, they can breathe in with a lot of tension and out lightly and vice versa. They can make up 'breathing' patterns in twos.

(iii) The children grow bigger as before and when the teacher says, 'now' they run, leap, twirl, spin as lightly as they can and settle back down on the floor again. They repeat this without any assistance from the teacher, working to their individual rhythms, bringing out the tension in the getting bigger and the lightness in the 'flying about the room'.

(iv) The children practise light flicking movements as if playing with a balloon. They imagine they are keeping the balloon up in the air by patting it gently. They travel all over the room, making light patting movements with the hands. They can then try making similar movements lightly with other parts of the body. The children can make up light flicking patterns using different body parts and flicking in different directions.

(v) The children can practise strong jumps to represent the balloon bursting or trying to burst a balloon. They can jump and clap their hands above their heads. Let them try to jump and clap their hands in different places, behind their backs or under one leg, for example. They can make up strong jumpy patterns.

(vi) Let the children choose two or three of the above ideas and develop their own 'balloon' dances to the music. They could work in pairs, to make up a 'balloon' dance.

Class Dance

(i) The children start lying on the floor. When the music starts they do their 'breathing' patterns which they worked out in task (ii).

(ii) When the teacher bangs a cymbal they twirl, spin, leap etc. lightly all over the room and then settle back on the floor near a partner.

(iii) They do their partner dances made up in task (vi).

(iv) When the teacher bangs the cymbal, they do a series of strong jumps and end up in a circle.

(v) The teacher bangs the cymbal five times and the children grow up slowly, keeping together like one big balloon.

(vi) The teacher then gives the cymbal one final big bang and the children run, jump, twirl and spin gradually dying down till they finish lying on the floor in a space.

Criteria for the evaluation of this unit of work

(i) Do the children appreciate that movements can be performed with strength or lightly?

(ii) Are they aware that movements performed with strength convey a different feeling from those performed lightly?

(iii) Did they understand the process of using a balloon as a stimulus and interpreting the way it behaved through movement?

(iv) Does anything need to be changed?

YEAR 2 CLASSES

Sample 1

Area of Activity: Dance.
Unit of Work: Moving on different levels.
Title of Dance: *The Secret Garden*.
Learning Intentions: Help children to understand the concepts of high and low, near to and far away in dance.
Music required: Tristan's 'Magic Garden' by Sky.
Development of Dance over six weeks
Select from the following ideas, try to get a balance in the lessons. Discuss a secret garden and what it might contain.

(i) Practise running and jumping. Pretend to be jumping OVER something, getting knees really high. As you jump say, 'OVER' in a high squeaky voice. Pretend to step OVER big rocks stretching the legs high. Step backwards as well as forwards.

Some children make low shapes near the floor for the rest to step OVER very carefully.

(ii) Find ways of sliding along the floor.
Try to wriggle as you slide.
Talk about sliding 'commando' fashion. As you wriggle or slide say, 'UNDERNEATH' in a deep growly voice, and pretend to slide under something.
Some children make bridges with their bodies.
The rest slide UNDER the bridges.

(iii) Sitting down on the floor with hands wide apart draw them closely NEAR to each other. How NEAR can you get your hands without touching? Make a magic space between your hands. Walk about keeping that magic space. Blow into that magic space and blow your hands FAR APART.

(iv) Repeat with other parts of your body, for example, a hand and a knee, a foot and an elbow etc.

(v) Find a partner and see how NEAR you can reach without touching. Can you reach with a knee, hand, foot, elbow?

(vi) Walk in and out of each other. How NEAR can you get without touching. How FAR AWAY can you run when the teacher claps her hands?

(vii) Practise reaching out and 'sticking' to someone close to you.

(viii) Make up a dance with your partner in which you go over and under each other. (Use slow, dreamy music)

(ix) Make up a dance in which you reach near to your partner with different parts of your body, find a good way of going far away from your partner.

(x) Put the two dances together to make one long one.

Class Dance

The secret of the garden is that all the children are invisible unless touched, in which case the spell is broken. The music is played throughout to help create the mystery of the garden.

(i) Children curl up in interesting shapes on the floor pretending to be asleep in the garden.

(ii)   Half the class wakes up, stretches and the children, finding themselves in a secret garden walk around exploring. They step carefully OVER all the 'curled up' shapes thinking they are rocks. They then make their bodies into bridges.

(iii) The rest of the class wakes up, stretches and slides gently UNDER all the bridges.

(iv)   All the children move about the garden being careful not to touch another child. Someone accidentally touches another child and the spell is broken. All the children become 'stuck' to one another, one foot is stuck to an elbow, a knee to a hand etc.

(v)   The teacher gives the magic word and the spell is broken. All the children run FAR AWAY back to their original places and go back to sleep.

Criteria for the evaluation of this unit of work

(i)   Do the children understand the concepts of 'high and low', 'near and far away'?

(ii)   Were they able to bring out the expressive nature of the movements?

(iii) Could they create an air of mystery in the magic garden?

(iv)   Does anything need to be changed?

Sample 2

Area of Activity: Dance.
Unit of Work: Moving in different directions.
Title of Dance: Cuckoo Clocks
Learning Intentions: To experience moving from side to side in a rocking action, spiralling, learning to do crouch jumps in different directions.
Music required: 'Time' by Pink Floyd.
Selected pieces of electronic music.
Development of Dance over six weeks
Select from the following ideas. Try to get a balance in the lessons. Discuss the components of a clock, look at examples. This could tie in with a topic on clocks and telling the time.

(i)   Find different ways of rocking from one part of the body to another. Choose different positions, for example, sitting, lying, kneeling, standing etc. Rock to the words:

> Tick tock, tick tock, goes the cuckoo clock
> As it stands upon the ground,
> The pendulum swings to and fro
> And the hands go round and round.

(ii)   Pretend you have a piece of chalk in your hand. Draw a big circle in the air in front of you. Then draw a circle to one side of you and to the other side. Try to draw a circle behind you. Draw a circle above your head. Now circle your arms like the hands of a clock.

(iii) Hold hands in a long line with a leader. Can the children follow the leader all over the room without letting go of their hands?

(iv)   In lines of six or seven children play follow-my-leader games.

(v)   Learn to do crouch jumps (or bunny hops). Remember to put the hands down first and then jump the feet up to the hands. Keep arms straight, and legs tucked up. Look behind you to make sure you do not kick anyone.

(vi)   In groups of three or four children make up some movements to represent a grandfather or cuckoo clock, two could rock like a pendulum, one could circle the arms like the hands of the clock and one rotate slowly like a cog wheel.

Class Dance

(i)   To the music, the children in their groups perform movements that represent either a grandfather or cuckoo clock.

(ii)   The teacher bangs a cymbal and the clocks break into pieces. The children scatter and fall down.

(iii) To music — one group gets together and the children circle their arms. These are all the hands of the clocks that have met to decide what to do.

103

(iv)   Another group gets together and rocks from side to side representing the pendulums.

(v)   A third group travel about in different directions doing crouch jumps (bunny hops) and saying, 'cuckoo, cuckoo' as they jump.

(vi)   They all then join hands and make a spiral led by the teacher. The spiral gets tighter and tighter representing a spring being wound up.

(vii)   When the spring cannot get any tighter it breaks. Children run back to their initial groups and start to move again like they did at the beginning to show that all the clocks are happily mended.

Criteria for the evaluation of this unit of work

(i)   Do the children understand a rocking action and did they have a range of ways of doing this?

(ii)   Were they able to create group 'clocks?'

(iii)   Did they understand that the selected movements represented the movements of a clock?

(iv)   Did they come up with any good ideas of their own?

(v)   Does anything need to be changed?

Useful music for dance

Space Odyssey (2001)	Deodata
The Pink Panther Theme	Mancini
Big Suspense Movie Themes	Geoff Love
Hary Janos Suite	Kodaly
Carnival of the Animals	Saint Saëns
Pictures at an Exhibition	Mussorgsky, arranged by Tomita
The Dark Side of the Moon	Pink Floyd
Snowflakes are Falling	Arranged by Tomita
Firebird	Arranged by Tomita
Equinoxe	Jean Michel Jarre
Sky 2	John Williams
20 All Time Junior Hits	Various
Greatest Hits Hooked on Classics	Original Recordings
Novels for the Moons	Axxess
Heaven and Hell	Vangelis
The Snowman	Howard Blake
Tubular Bells	Mike Oldfield
Cats	Andrew Lloyd Webber
Songs for Annie	John Galway
BBC Sporting Themes	Various

Chapter Six

Swimming in the Early Years

Introduction

Why include swimming in the PE programme?

The earlier children gain confidence in water the better. Many adults trying to learn to swim do not like water on their faces, are afraid to put their heads under the water and are so tense that they are unable to relax, affecting the ability to float.

Most children do not have the same fear of the water because they have not had any previous negative experiences that deter adults. It is important that all activities for children are fun, building up and maintaining their confidence.

Children who can swim will be able to survive if they get into difficulties. All governing bodies of water sports demand an ability to swim before taking part, so older children who cannot swim are denied the chance to do exciting activities such as canoeing, windsurfing and sailing.

Swimming is a very popular leisure activity for all the family; most public pools are busy all the year round. Swimming is a good way to get fit and stay fit. Propulsion through the water requires strength and stamina and all the body is involved in the action helping to keep the joints flexible. Controlled breathing helps develop the lungs which makes swimming a particularly valuable exercise for those with asthma.

Surveys (Hardy, Lee *et al.*) have shown that children learning to swim gain a great deal of self-esteem and this has an influence, albeit temporarily, on other curriculum areas. This is because it is a distinctly measurable activity and the children know when they have succeeded. They may receive badges and certificates to prove it, but these are not necessary, the intrinsic sense of achievement is what counts to the child.

Psychological values in learning to swim have been listed as:

> 'an appreciation of personal success, giving a sense of achievement;
> an improvement in self-image and a development of independence;
> a sense of physical well-being which may help confidence and poise;
> an improvement in self-discipline.' (Harrison, 1989)

General considerations

Swimming must be fun. This means warm water and surroundings in which the children feel confident. Adults will be needed in the water to assist. They should be told how best to do this and have an idea in advance of the activities the teacher is going to do with the children. Although they do not need to be competent swimmers, the adult helpers must not mind being splashed and getting their hair wet. The class teacher needs to be on the pool side where she can see everybody and the children can see a familiar face. She needs to be prepared to enter the water if necessary and this means wearing suitable clothing.

Moving through water is a very different

experience for children at first. Confidence can be gained through free play and the playing of simple games. Beginners will be more confident if wearing arm bands and the teacher also may feel happier if she knows they have this means of support.

The water should be shallow enough for them to stand up in and they should be encouraged to use all the available space and not hug the sides of the pool. They should be set an activity as soon as they enter the water.

A child who is reluctant to go into the water should be invited to sit on the side and watch, perhaps dangling his feet in the water. He should not be forced in any way.

Any child beginning to shiver should leave the water and get dressed under the supervision of an adult. Getting cold can lead to hypothermia.

Safety procedures should be explained beforehand and followed at all times. Although swimming should be fun, this does not mean the lessons are unstructured and children feel safer when they know exactly what to do. Clear, simple instructions should be given and the children also need opportunity to try things out for themselves and consolidate what they have achieved. There should be a great deal of repetition to establish ways of moving through water and to build confidence.

Kick boards or floats are very useful and if these can be obtained in different colours, (for example, red, blue, green and yellow) it helps with the organization of groups. Plastic toys such as ducks, can be used by the children to play with in the water, or as markers on the pool side to indicate progress when learning to swim.

Swimming lessons vary slightly from other activities. The tasks will be much more directed and less open-ended. It is easy to see the level of ability of each child and in order not to have too many children in the water at once, it is probably best to group them. Therefore the activities which will be outlined in this chapter will depend on the ability of the children rather than their age.

Although the National Curriculum Physical Education Statutory Orders make swimming an optional activity at Key Stage 1, this is the best time to teach the children if possible and much of the Programmes of Study for Key Stage 2 outlined for swimming is appropriate, in particular:

> 'Pupils should be taught:
> (b) to develop confidence in water, and how to rest, float and adopt support positions;
> (c) a variety of means of propulsion using either arms or legs or both, and how to develop effective and efficient strokes on the front and the back.'
> (National Curriculum PE)

Safety considerations

The safety of the children must be observed at all times. If the children swim at a local public pool, the safety procedures will be established for the general public but nevertheless the classteacher has overall responsibility for the children in her care. Obviously it is best if the teacher is a fully qualified swimming teacher and life-saver, and it is essential that only an adult holding a relevant and current life-saving qualification should teach children swimming in deep water.

The teacher must be able to enter the pool and wade in to a child in difficulties if necessary, and should be able to administer basic life support in the form of mouth-to-mouth resuscitation.

Before entering the water the children should leave their clothes neatly in the right place, visit the toilet, blow their noses, wear caps if they have long hair, and wash their feet in the foot bath. They should not swim immediately after a meal and must not chew sweets or gum in the water.

Children should be reminded not to run or push another child, not to shout, not to enter the water until told, to stand still if they hear a whistle, to do exactly what they are told.

The teacher should count the children on

entry into the water, during the session and as they leave the water.

A long pole should be available to reach a child if necessary.

There should be a telephone within easy reach and an emergency number clearly displayed nearby.

Pupil-teacher ratios vary from one local authority to another, but the numbers must be kept reasonably small in the early years and should not exceed twenty to one. A child who has epilepsy must have an adult supervising that child only.

Emergency action

Accidents do sometimes occur and when they do, they can happen quickly. A child in difficulties tends not to struggle and, unless the teacher is very observant, may not be noticed immediately.

A child who is conscious needs to be taken out of the water. He can be reached by hand or with a pole, or a rope thrown to him to hang on to.

The unconscious child needs to be removed from the water quickly. Speed is essential. He should be brought to the surface and resuscitation begun as soon as possible, either by supporting him at the pool side whilst still in the water, or immediately after landing.

Basic life support

The child should be laid on his back, and checks made to see if he is breathing. If not, his mouth should be inspected for obstructions, and his head tilted backwards. His nose should be pinched and the teacher should seal his mouth with hers, and she should blow gently and steadily ten times into his mouth, at a rate of one-and-a-half times per second, checking that the chest rises and falls. If breathing has not restarted then this should be continued until help arrives.

This is a very brief outline of what to do and it is strongly recommended that all teachers should learn first aid.

Curriculum content — areas of experience the children should have in swimming

Beginners

For beginners the areas of experience include entering the water safely and confidently, how to leave the water, getting the face wet, getting the feeling of going under the water and knowing how to resurface, beginning to move through the water and learning to do the strokes.

Entry into shallow water

These activities are graded. At least one adult should be in the water, the class teacher must be on the pool side.

(i)   An adult enters the water first showing the children how to walk down the steps backwards, looking down to see where to place the foot on each step. The child follows knowing the adult is at the bottom of the steps to receive him.

(ii)   The children walk down the steps one after the other unaided. The more competent children going first.

(iii)   An adult enters the water, the child sits on the side with his feet in the water. He puts his hands on the adult's shoulders and the adult supports him by placing her hands on his waist. The adult lifts him into the water. (Particularly useful for pre-school children and very timid children.)

(iv)   The children sit on the side, place their hands on one side of their bodies, fingers facing backwards. They slide into the water, feet first, turning as they do so to face the wall.

(v) An adult stands in the water, arms out-stretched towards each child who is standing on the side. The child jumps into the adult's arms.

(vi) Children jump in unaided. Their feet MUST enter the water first.

(vii) The children turn in the air as they jump in.

(viii) The children enter via the steps one at a time. They turn on the bottom step to face the water. They push off with their feet, arms outstretched and glide away from the step along the surface of the water into the arms of an adult.

(ix) The children push and glide as before unaided, starting to swim at the end of the glide.

(x) The children push and glide as before on a higher step each time.

Leaving the water

(i) Children leave by climbing up the steps followed closely by an adult.

(ii) The children climb up the steps unaided.

(iii) The children face the pool side, place both hands firmly on the side, jump up and turn to sit on the side facing the water.

Getting the face wet

Tell the children to:

(i) wash their hands, arms, tummies, faces and hair in the water;

(ii) dip their noses in the water;

(iii) draw patterns in the water with their fingers and then their noses;

(iv) cup their hands and fill with water, blow the water away;

(v) cup their hands, fill with water, wash their faces;

(vi) hold the rail or pool side, put their faces in the water;

(vii) hold the rail as before, put their faces in the water and blow bubbles;

(viii) hold rail as before, put their faces in the water, open their eyes and look at their toes;

(ix) play 'The Weather Game'. Each child has a float which he holds tightly in both hands. When the teachers says, 'Rough sea' the children make waves by moving the float from side to side in front of them. When she says, 'It's raining' they scoop water over their heads with the float. When she says, 'It's thundering' they smack their floats on the surface of the water.

Submerging and surfacing

When introducing submerging tell the children to take a big breath and then try the following activities, but do not forget to tell them how to resurface, i.e. put their feet on the bottom of the pool and push themselves back up to the surface. On surfacing try to discourage rubbing the eyes.

Tell the children to:

(i) stand, holding the rail or side, duck under the water;

(ii) hold an adult's hand (or partner's hand) and duck under the water;

(iii) stand in a space and duck under;

(iv) touch the bottom of the pool with the finger tips and then both hands;

(v) kneel, touch the bottom of the pool with the finger tips and then both hands;

(vi) kneel on the bottom of the pool. Then put feet on bottom of the pool to stand;

(vii) sit on the bottom of the pool;

(viii) pick up weighted sticks and rings off the bottom;

(ix) jump up in the air and then submerge;

(x) play, 'Ring a Ring O' Roses' and 'Pop! Goes the Weasel' with an adult and other children.

Moving through the water

Children should wear armbands at first. Encourage them to work away from the side or rail. Have an adult in the water with them in case a child loses his balance. Emphasize how to stand up, i.e. push the feet down firmly onto the bottom, raise the head, push down with the hands.

Moving with the feet on the bottom of the pool
Tell the children to:

(i)   place a plastic toy in the water so that it floats. Walk away from it and towards it;
(ii)   walk freely about the pool, sliding their feet along the bottom;
(iii) walk about, shoulders just under the water, arms stretched out with the arm bands resting on top of the water;
(iv)   walk about as before in circles, zig-zags, squares, going backwards;
(v)   walk to meet a partner. Walk with a partner, holding hands;
(vi)   walk behind a partner, hands on the shoulders of the child in front;
(vii) face a partner, one walks forwards and one backwards, holding hands;
(viii) walk, taking big steps, little steps, on tiptoes, legs crossed;
(ix)   jump, hop, and skip in the water. Try with a partner, both doing the same;
(x)   imagine walking through treacle, pushing and pulling with the hands;
(xi)   imagine walking up a hill, leaning slightly forward;
(xii) in a line with four or five children, hands on the shoulders of the child in front, 'follow-my-leader' all over the pool;
(xiii) in a line as before but without touching, copy what the leader does;
(xiv) in a circle, holding hands, play 'Pop! Goes the Weasel' — i.e. walk round saying the rhyme, jump up high on the word 'Pop';
(xv)   the teacher will say, 'walk', 'skip', 'hop' or 'run' and when she says 'Now' the

children stand still balancing a float on their heads.

Getting the feet off the bottom of the pool
These tasks are graded. The children should wear arm bands. There should be an adult in the water to help children regain standing if necessary. Tell the children to:

(i)   Stand alone in the water, arms resting lightly on the surface in front of the body, feel the arm bands floating. Try to press them down under the water. See how hard it is;
(ii)   walk, taking big steps, pushing the legs backwards and upwards behind the body;
(iii) leaning on the arm bands with arms outstretched in front of the body, push one leg back as before then change legs before putting the other foot down;
(iv)   hold the side of the pool, let the legs float up behind the body;
(v)   hold the side of the pool, kick the legs up and down in the water;
(vi)   walk anywhere holding a float out in front of the body;
(vii) walk taking big steps, holding a float, letting the free leg come up behind the body as in (ii);
(viii) holding a float, gently let the legs come off the bottom of the pool;
(ix)   holding a float, gently let the legs come off the bottom, kick them as many times as possible before pressing them down hard in order to stand up;
(x)   hold the float out in front of the body, lift one leg behind the body, push off with the other leg and glide forwards through the water;
(xi)   place one float under each arm so that it lies flat on the water;
       Lean on the floats like leaning on the arms of a big arm chair. Lift one knee out of the water in front of the body. Then push the leg down hard, lift the head, press down on the floats to stand up. Repeat lifting the other knee;

(xii)   repeat (xi) but lift both knees at once so that the body is sitting in the water, like sitting in a big arm chair. Practise several times, especially how to stand up;

(xiii) repeat (xii) but once the knees have been lifted, straighten out the body so that it is lying on the top of the water (on the back). Stand up as before.

(The advantage of (xii) and (xiii) is that the face is away from the water and the child can see the teacher at all times. Steps (xi), (xii) and (xiii) can be repeated lifting the knees behind the body instead of in front so that the child succeeds in lying just below the surface of the water on his front. If he can do this then he can begin to propel himself along by kicking his legs.)

(xiv)   push and glide and stand up holding a float;

(xv)   push, and glide towards the side without a float;

(xvi)   push, glide and stand up away from the side without a float;

(xvii) push, and glide with the face in the water, then stand up;

(xviii) push, and glide with the face in the water, paddle with the hands and then stand up;

(xix)   push, glide, paddle with the hands and kick the legs;

(xx)   repeat (xix). Place a plastic toy on the side of the pool; Swim along the side of the pool as far as the toy. Move the toy along a bit further each time;

(xxi)   Remove the arm bands (or let some of the air out of them) and repeat all the tasks.

The children will perform a 'doggy paddle' stroke at first. This does not matter. Some children like to sweep the water away with a kind of breaststroke action with the arms and kicking the legs. This is also acceptable as it achieves its aim of propelling the body through the water.

Many children will use the arms and forget the legs. This does not matter either. The biggest problem is the angle of the head. If it is held right out of the water it acts as a break and hinders propulsion and the legs tend to sink. Try to get the children to put their faces in the water as they swim. If they take a big breath they can swim until they need to stop for another breath.

Do not let them try to swim a specific distance such as a length of the pool until the stroke has improved enough for them to cover the distance easily and without strain, this means learning to incorporate a smooth breathing pattern into the stroke.

The teaching process

How to teach the strokes

Once the children can move through the water without arm bands, the strokes can be worked on to make the body more efficient and streamlined. Regular breathing patterns will help with swimming longer distances.

Children should try swimming on the back and on the front in every lesson so that the front crawl and back crawl are developed alongside each other. They have a great deal in common anyway, but some children will prefer one stroke to the other. A few will have a tendency to want to develop the breast stroke and this should be introduced as soon as the children can swim a width confidently. At first a child may swim with a breast stroke arm action and kick the legs up and down as in the front crawl, this is acceptable until it is obvious that the child is competent and ready to change to a more orthodox and effective way of swimming.

Most of the explanations of what to do should be made with the children staying in the water. Occasionally it may be necessary to show them the arm action of a stroke out of the water, but this should be kept to a minimum.

The children can watch demonstrations of good style from the side, observing the stroke as the swimmer performs it across the pool.

A brief description of each stroke follows so that the teacher knows what she is aiming for. However, for this age group it may be simpler for the children to look at the following, bearing in mind that a flat body position will help propulsion:

(i)   What we do with our arms when we swim.

(ii)   What we do with our legs when we swim.

(iii)   What we do with our heads when we swim.

(iv)   What we do to breathe easily when we swim.

The front crawl

Body position

Just under the surface, horizontal and streamlined. The head should be in line with the rest of the body. The eyes look to the bottom of the pool, with the water just above the forehead. 'Swim downhill'.

Leg action

Alternately kicking in an up and down movement, from the hips, toes pointed, with the legs almost straight. There should be a slight splashing with the feet to a depth of about twelve inches for children. Legs should be close together.

Arm action

The hand enters the water in advance of the head, finger nails going into the water first. The arm should be straight from finger nails to elbow. There should be no splash. The arm pulls down under the water and then pushes backwards towards the thigh. The arm then returns to the entry position clear of the water.

Breathing

The head turns to snatch a breath as the arm pulls through the water. The air is expelled as the arm recovers clear of the water by blowing bubbles in the water.

Teaching the stroke

Progression	*Teaching points*
1 *Body position* Push and glide from side	Stretch arms out, push off with feet, arms slide along surface (imagine you are sliding along the top of a polished table)
Repeat — how far can you go? Repeat — keep faces in water	If children find submerging difficult teach them to 'mushroom float' first, i.e. in an upright position, leaning forwards so that the head and shoulders are under water
2 *Leg action* Leg kick holding rail or side	Rather static so keep practice short. Small splash with heels breaking surface
Leg kick holding a float	Launch gently, keep arms extended, keep float horizontal holding it by the sides, thumbs on top

3 *Arm action*
   Standing, lean forwards, one foot in front | Hands firm, fingers together, finger nails en-
   of the other face in the water, hold breath | ter water first, elbows raised
4 *Breathing*
   Swim and breathe as necessary
   Practise blowing bubbles, breathing out
   under water
   Stand, shoulders under water, face in | Concentrate on turning the head sideways.
   water, breathe out and turn head side- | Turn to look at something beside you
   ways to breathe in
   Stand, hold float at diagonally opposite | Children should discover which side they pre-
   corners, turn head to put *ear* on float, i.e. | fer to turn their heads
   turn head to the left if the left hand is at
   the bottom of the float, then *nose* (turn to
   look at hand nearest to you)
   Repeat swimming — breathe in once and | Teach children to 'snatch' a breath under
   blow out every complete cycle | water
5 *Timing*
   Push and glide, bring in leg kick and arm | Teach three leg kicks to one arm pull, i.e.,
   action | kick, kick, kick, *kick*, kick, kick
   Swim as far as you can holding your
   breath
   Repeat breathing half way across the pool
   Repeat breathing once every six strokes
   Repeat breathing once every complete
   cycle
6 *Other activities*
   Try swimming in time with a partner | Encourage swimming slowly
   Count how many strokes you take to swim | Aim at being consistent
   a width or a length
   Use the pool clock — how far can you | You can use an egg-timer, stop watch or clock
   swim in one minute? | — keep time short to begin with
7 *Common faults*
   Body position — head too high in the
                    water due to fear of getting face wet
   Leg action   — kick is too deep
                    kick is too shallow — 'fluttering'
                    ankles are stiff
                    knees bent
   Arm action   — entry too flat causing splashing
                    wrists not firm enough
                    limb track incorrect — arms crossing central line on entry
   Breathing   — head lifted and not turned
   Timing   — arms and legs not coordinated, breathing irregular.

The back crawl

Body position

Extended horizontal position on the back — streamlining with the hips well up to the surface but not breaking it. Head in line with body, eyes looking upwards at an angle of forty-five degrees to the body.

Leg action

Alternating kick up and down starting from the hips, knees practically straight. Kick up. Depth of kick about 12″. Toes just approach surface so that small splash is made (identical to front crawl).

Arm action

Windmill action — one arm always opposite the other

Entry — hands enter water at 'five minutes to one' position, little finger first

Pull — the hand feels for a position in water so that body can be pulled past it. Wrist slightly flexed. Hand follows a sideways pathway till near thigh

Recovery — hand is taken from its propulsive phase, thumb leading, and returned to entry position (rule = little finger in, thumb out)

Breathing

Face out of water so no problem
Once or twice every stroke

Timing

Six leg beats to one arm cycle
Opposite leg kicks downwards to arm

Teaching the stroke

Progression	Teaching points
1 **Body position** Push and glide on back from pool side and then stand up	Check children know how to regain standing
2 **Leg action** Leg kick using two floats, one under each arm	Start standing and launch gently on to back by bending knees and rolling backwards as if rolling over a barrel behind you
Leg kick hugging float on chest	Keep hips up to touch float as if cuddling a teddy bear
Leg kick sculling with hands	Hands paddle backwards and forwards at sides, i.e. towards and away from hips. Travel head first
Push and glide, add arm and leg action	
3 **Arm action** Standing Push and glide, add arm action half way across the pool	One foot in front of the other, shoulders under water. A static practice so keep short
Leg action half way across pool then arm action Scull half way across pool then add arm action	Launch body gently and start carefully without splashing

4 *Breathing*

Breathe in as arm is raised and out when it is under water, or breathe in for three strokes and out for three strokes

Breathing is no problem as face is out of water all the time, but make children conscious of a regular breathing pattern

5 *Timing*

Whole stroke practice — six leg kicks to one arm cycle

i.e. *Kick* kick kick, *kick* kick kick

<table>
<tr><td>1</td><td>2</td><td>3</td><td>1</td><td>2</td><td>3</td></tr>
<tr><td colspan="3">left arm</td><td colspan="3">right arm</td></tr>
</table>

6 *Other activities*

Try keeping in time with a partner

Swim slowly

Count how many strokes you need to swim a width or a length

Try to be consistent

How far can you swim in one minute?

Time with an oven-timer, stop watch, alarm clock etc. if no pool clock available

7 *Common faults*

Body position — head too far back in water hips too low in water

Leg action — poor leg kick — fluttering or twitching, 'cycling' action with feet kicking with flat feet instead of extended toes and relaxed ankles

Arm action — hands too wide on entry
hands pausing at thighs
back of hand entering water first

Timing — arms and legs not coordinated causing rolling

Sculling

(i) Sculling is used with the back crawl leg action to propel, balance and control the body on the back.

(ii) Arms are close to the body, hands by the hips, elbows as straight as possible.

(iii) The hands should be firm and flat with fingers together.

(iv) The hands move inwards and outwards at the wrists, making a figure of eight pattern.

(v) The thumbs draw the first half of the figure of 8 on the outward movement and on the inward movement, the little finger draws the second half.

(vi) Smooth continuous pivoting from the wrists will assist balance and propulsion.

The breast stroke

Body position

Just under surface, streamlined and symmetric, head slightly higher to keep feet under surface, face forward and clear of surface.

Leg action (consists of two parts — recovery, and propulsion)

Recovery — From extended position, heels drawn up close to seat about hip width apart

Propulsion— Feet driven backwards and slightly outwards, being brought together in one smooth movement — kick with heels, maintain cocked position of feet as long as possible. Propulsion is gained from driving backwards with feet. Width of kick unimportant

Arm action (hands under water throughout)

Propulsion — From extended position, palms down, the hands are pulled sideways and downwards to a depth of about 12″

Recovery — Elbows tucked in close to chest, hands pass forward under chin.

Palms may turn upwards but turn down ready for next propulsive movement

of pull. Breathe out by 'blowing' the hands back to the extended position.

Breathing

If head is above surface there is no problem. One breath per arm action, breathing in at end

Timing

Continuous alternation — arms take over from legs. There is a delay between end of arm action and beginning of leg kick.

Teaching the stroke

Progressions	Teaching points
1 *Body position* Push and glide from side, stand	Check children know how to stand from a prone position
2 *Leg action* Leg kick at rail	Check body is symmetric Kick with the heels. Feet are turned up Feet snap together, soles uppermost
Leg kick across pool holding float Repeat, reducing the number of leg kicks needed to cross pool	Check kick is symmetrical, arms extended forwards
3 *Arm action* Standing, shoulders in water	Arms extended *pull* downwards then *tuck* fingers in under chin (like a dog begging for a biscuit). *Stretch* arms out Pull, tuck, stretch
Arm action walking	
4 *Breathing* Arm action, walking and breathing	Inhale on pull, exhale on stretch — blow fingers away from chin
Whole stroke	Concentrate on breathing with arm action as above
5 *Timing* Whole stroke	Demonstrate on pool side using one leg (standing on the other) and arms
On pool side using arms and one leg (stand on the other) In water — whole stroke — (imagine you are swimming through a tunnel)	Show how to *pull* with arms and legs and *stretch* arms as legs snap together
6 *Other activities* Try keeping in time with a partner How few strokes do you need to swim a length? How far can you swim in a minute?	Swim slowly This helps with streamlining Use oven-timer, stop watch, egg timer alarm clock if no pool clock is available

Try swimming on your back and doing the breast stroke leg action inverted, and scull with your hands

Children can see what their legs are doing

7 *Common faults*

Body position — head held too high
body too low — swimming under water
Leg action — 'screw kick' — not symmetric
not kicking with the heels
kick too wide — tell children to swim as close to the pool side as possible
Arm action — pulling too wide — outwards and not downwards enough
hands not stretched forwards in recovery hands break surface
Breathing — swimmers hold breath
Timing — arms and legs not coordinated

Some water games for infants

(i)   Here We Go Round the Mulberry Bush
Children hold hands in circles of six.
They walk round singing, 'Here we go Round the Mulberry Bush, the Mulberry Bush, the Mulberry Bush. Here we go Round the Mulberry Bush on a cold and frosty morning.'

When they sing, 'on a cold and frosty morning' they let go of their hands, hug themselves and shiver.

They then sing the following three verses, doing the corresponding actions:
'This is the way we wash our hands'
'This is the way we clap our hands'
'This is the way we jump up high'

(ii) Humpty Dumpty
Children hold hands in circles of six.
They walk round singing, 'Humpty Dumpty sat on a wall'.

They let go of their hands and duck under the water as they sing, 'Humpty Dumpty had a great fall'.

They then walk anywhere singing, 'All the King's horses and all the King's men' and rejoin their circles on the words, 'Couldn't put Humpty together again'. They do a big jump on the word, 'again'.

(iii) Frogs and Fishes (a follow-my-leader game)
In pairs, one child is a frog and the other is a fish. If the teacher calls out, 'Frog' the fish has to copy what the frog does. If the teacher calls out, 'Fish' the frog has to copy what the fish does. When the teacher calls out, 'A big wave is coming', the children have to leave their partners and find new ones but they must find someone who is different from them, i.e. a frog must partner a fish.

(iv) Busy Bee
In pairs, the teacher will call out different parts of the body, i.e. 'head to head' and the children have to stand with their heads touching. Or she might say, 'back to back' and they have to stand with their backs touching, and so on. When she calls out, 'Busy Bee' they have to buzz off and find a new partner.

(v)   Find the Treasure
Anything that floats (i.e. arm bands, rubber rings, plastic ducks, kick boards etc.) is placed in the water and is the treasure. The children have to walk in and out of the treasure without touching it. The teacher then calls out, 'Find some red treasure' and the children hold up something red. Or she might say, 'Find some

round treasure' and they have to hold up something round, etc. When she calls out, 'The coastguard's coming' all the treasure has to be hidden under the water.

(vi)   Sausages

The teacher calls out instructions such as, 'hop', 'skip', 'run' or 'jump' and the children do the corresponding actions. When she calls out 'sausages' followed by a number, the children have to line up one behind the other with their hands on the shoulders of the child in front of them to make a string of sausages. Each string of sausages is made up by the right number of children, for example, if she says, 'sausages, five' children form lines of five.

The planning process

This will take place at three levels. In the first instance the school will have an overall planning statement which will identify the needs of the children and how these needs will be met. Swimming is a skill-based activity and the lessons will depend on the level of skill of the children. Therefore the planning will take a slightly different form from other areas of activity and instead of planning for each year group, each ability group will need to be catered for.

Overall planning

The planning statement will be concise. The aim is obviously to get the children swimming with good style. However, the school will need to look at how this is to be done and identify the access to a pool, whether outside instruction is available, costs and organization.

Year planning

This will depend on how much swimming the children are going to receive. It may be that just Year 2 children will go swimming and the planning will be more directed towards organization of the groups to make best possible use of the available time.

Planning by the classteacher

Again this will be organizational planning at first. However, if the children are organized in small groups, then lesson plans will need to be prepared by whoever teaches each group.

Lesson structure

Warming up

The children need to begin by getting familiar with being in the water, to listening to the teacher and getting wet all over. As soon as they enter the water they should be given a task which should involve, if possible, keeping them away from the pool side. They could be given an instruction such as, 'See if you can walk in and out of everybody without touching the side of the pool'.

This should be followed by some play-like activities based on getting the face and hair wet.

Development

The teacher will concentrate on one aspect of learning to swim depending on the level of ability. She will give the children opportunities to go on their backs and fronts, and change the activity fairly frequently to hold their interest.

If the children can swim, they should practise the whole stroke before concentrating on one aspect of the stroke, and then go back to the whole stroke again before going on to another stroke.

Free choice

The children should have a chance to choose what they want to do for a few minutes to consolidate what they have learnt.

Conclusion

This can be in the form of a simple game such as 'Ring a Ring O' Roses', a challenge such as trying to pick objects off the bottom, or standing

117

on a float without falling off. They could try to float on their backs in a star shape whilst the teacher counts up to ten which would help to calm them down before getting out of the water.

Evaluating the success of the swimming programme

This should not be difficult because the progress made is easily observable and measurable.

The aim outlined in the overall planning statement is to teach children to swim competently and the success will depend on how confident the children are in the water, how many have learnt to swim and how much improvement has been made by those who could already swim.

The basis for evaluating the success of the swimming programme can be the National Curriculum Statement:

> 'pupils should be taught:
> (b) a variety of means of propulsion using either arms or legs or both, and to develop effective and efficient strokes on the front and the back.' (National Curriculum PE)

There are various swimming awards that can be given to children when they have achieved recognized milestones in swimming. Some local authorities have their own award schemes or the school may have its own system. This is left to the discretion of the school who may not necessarily agree with awards. Badges and certificates prove to adults that the child has achieved a recognized standard.

SAMPLE UNITS OF WORK FOR EACH ABILITY GROUP

Sample 1: BEGINNERS
Area of Activity: Swimming.
Unit of Work: Developing confidence in the water.
Relevant National Curriculum PE Statement: Pupils should be taught to develop confidence in water.

Learning Intentions: To help children to move through the water confidently.
Development over six lessons
Children will wear arm bands at first. They will be taught the codes of hygiene and courtesy when using swimming pools. There will be adult help in the water.

(i)   Children enter pool by steps.
        Children play with a plastic toy in the water.
        Children will 'wash' the toy and then place it on the side.
        Children will 'wash' their arms, hands, tummies and faces in the water.
        They will walk anywhere sliding their feet on the bottom.
        They will jump up and down.
        They will play 'Pop Goes the Weasel', jumping up on the word 'pop'.

(ii)   Children will follow the same procedure as last lesson.
        They will place the toy in the water away from them and walk up to it and away from it.
        They will draw pictures in the water with their noses.
        They will blow bubbles in the water.

(iii)   Children will follow the same procedure as last lesson, but without any toys.
        They will hop, jump and run in the water.
        They will play the 'animal game', i.e. run when the teacher calls out monkeys, 'hop' when the teacher calls out rabbits and 'jump' when the teacher calls out kangaroos.
        They will walk taking big steps lifting the free leg high behind them.

(iv)   Children will play the 'animal game'.
        They will draw pictures in the water with their noses and blow bubbles.
        They will walk taking big steps.
        They will hold the side and let their legs float up, learning how to stand up from a floating position.
        They will hold a float and let their legs float up.

(v)   Children will play the 'animal game'.
They will hold the side and let their legs float up.
They will hold a float and let their legs float up.
They will have one float under each arm and 'sit' as if in an arm chair.
They will play, 'Ring a Ring O' Roses'.

(vi) Children will play the 'weather game' using floats (see page 108).
They will 'sit' in the water with a float under each arm and then try to straighten out on their backs and kick their legs.
They will try to kick their legs holding one float, going on their tummies.

(vii) Children will play the 'weather game'.
They will duck under the water and look at their toes.
They will kick their legs using a float.
They will kick their legs without a float, paddling with their hands.
They will play 'Pop goes the Weasel' and 'Ring a Ring O' Roses'.

Criteria for the evaluation of this unit of work

(i)   Can they put their faces in the water?
(ii) Can they move about the pool with confidence?
(iii) Can they move through the water without touching the bottom, wearing arm bands?
(iv) Does anything need to be changed?

Sample 2: IMPROVERS
Area of Activity: Swimming.
Unit of Work: Improving children's swimming strokes.
Relevant National Curriculum PE Statement:
Pupils should be taught a variety of means of propulsion using either arms or legs or both.
Learning Intentions: To improve the swimming strokes.
Development over six lessons
Children will be able to swim at least half a width without arm bands. Although they will focus on one aspect of the stroke each lesson,

they will swim the whole stroke most of the time.

(i)   What we do with our arms when we swim.
Children will practise 'doggy paddle'.
They will learn the arm action for front crawl.
They will learn to use the hands as paddles as in sculling.
They will try the arm action, 'like a frog' as in breast stroke.
They will play the 'weather game' (see sample 1).

(ii) What we do with our arms when we swim — continued.
The children will practise all they learnt in lesson (i).
They will learn to move their arms 'like a windmill' as in back crawl.
They will play 'water relay', i.e. in pairs, one each side of the pool.
'A' has a float and swims across to 'B' who swims back with the float.
The first one back is the winner.

(iii) What we do with our legs when we swim.
The children will practise the leg action for front crawl using floats.
They will practise the leg action for back crawl whilst sculling.
They will 'swim like a frog' using floats.
They will practise floating on their backs in a star shape.

(iv) What we do with our legs when we swim — continued.
The children will practise what they learnt in lessons (i), (ii) and (iii).
They will practise the leg action for back crawl.
They will float on their tummies.
They will try 'turning pancakes', i.e. float on tummies and turn over onto their backs without touching the bottom, keeping in a star shape.

(v)   What we do with our arms and legs when we swim.
The children will practise what they learn in lessons (i)–(iv).

They will concentrate on coordinating the arms and legs in front crawl and back crawl.

They will try to coordinate the arms and legs in the breast stroke.

They will learn to jump into the water from the pool side.

They will practise 'turning pancakes'.

(vi) <u>What we do with our arms and legs when we swim — continued.</u>

They will practise all they have learnt in lessons (i)–(v).

They will concentrate on coordinating the arms and legs in front crawl, back crawl and breast stroke.

They will jump into the water making different body shapes in the air.

They will pick up objects from the bottom of the pool.

They will play 'water relay'.

Criteria for the evaluation of this unit of work

(i) Are they more aware of what their arms do when they swim?

(ii) Are they more aware of what their legs do when they swim?

(iii) Can they jump in confidently?

(iv) Can they turn 'pancakes' in the water?

(v) Does anything need to be changed?

Sample 3: SWIMMERS

Area of Activity: Swimming.

Unit of Work: Helping children to develop effective and efficient swimming strokes on front and back.

Learning Intentions: Children will learn to streamline their strokes, and how to breathe correctly whilst swimming.

Development over six lessons

Children in this group will be able to swim a width unaided on their fronts and backs.

(i) Children will take a deep breath and try to swim as far as possible with the face in the water. They will stop when necessary and take another breath.

They will practise swimming making their bodies as flat as possible.

They will practise blowing bubbles in the water.

They will swim with a float, faces in the water, turning their heads to one side every fourth leg kick (front crawl leg action).

They will swim with a float under one arm and swim with the other arm, trying to watch the fingers of that arm all the time.

They will find a way of swimming with a partner, both holding on to the float.

(ii) The children will practise all the tasks in lesson (i).

They will practise front crawl, with the face in the water, turning the head every fourth stroke.

As they turn their heads they will snatch a breath and breathe out by blowing bubbles with their faces in the water.

They will practise back crawl keeping the body flat, eyes looking upwards and slightly forwards, chins tucked in.

They will practise breast stroke.

(iii) The children will practise all the tasks in lesson (ii).

They will work on turning the head and snatching a breath every fourth stoke of the front crawl.

They will practise back crawl, breathing in on the first arm cycle and out on the second.

They will practise a 'push and glide' from the pool side, keeping the body flat.

(iv) Children will practise all the tasks in lesson (iii).

They will try to coordinate the breathing with one arm cycle in the front crawl.

They will learn to breathe correctly in the breast stroke, keeping their heads out of the water.

They will 'push and glide' from the pool side trying to glide as far as possible.

They will learn to glide through a partner's legs.

(v) The children will practise front crawl, back crawl and breast stroke concentrating on a regular breathing pattern and flat body position.

They will learn to do a handstand in the water.

(vi) The children will practise their strokes as in lesson (v).

They will practise doing handstands.

They will learn to do somersaults in the water.

They will make up a way of swimming with a partner, using a float which they must both hold on to.

They will play simple games using a large plastic ball.

Criteria for the evaluation of this unit of work

(i) Are they beginning to swim in a stream-lined and efficient manner?

(ii) Have they mastered smooth, regular breathing patterns?

(iii) Has each stroke improved?

(iv) Does anything need to be changed?

Chapter Seven

Implementing a Whole School Policy in Physical Education in the Early Years

Introduction

Why have a whole school policy?

At one time each teacher taught physical education to her own class in isolation to what was being taught in the rest of the school. In order to ensure both balance and progression it is necessary for teachers to work together. This is particularly important in physical education because of the transient nature of the subject and the need to have a policy on safety which everyone follows.

The Education (Schools) Act of 1992 has required primary schools to be regularly inspected and there are DFE circulars and guidance on the legislation on which the inspections are to be based.

Although the reason for drawing up a school policy is for the ultimate benefit of the children, the fact that it is now compulsory by law also gives added weight to the importance of having a well-documented curriculum in physical education which spells out in writing what the teachers have been doing in the past and are doing and plan to do in the future, all pulling together in a unified way so that the children get continuity from one class to the next.

What should a school policy contain?

(i) A statement which outlines the rationale for physical education within the school.
(ii) Overall planning — the needs of the chil-dren and how these needs will be met, through schemes of work based on the programmes of study and the end of Key Stage Descriptions as outlined in the National Curriculum.
(iii) Units of work outlining the work to be covered during the school year.
(iv) Lesson plans.

A school curriculum statement for physical education

Points to be considered:

(i) The general ethos of the school regarding the value and importance it places on physical education.
(ii) The purpose of physical education — why teach it?
Considerations should be given to:
(a) the value of learning how to use the body effectively and efficiently in a range of different physical situations;
(b) how much importance the school puts on the learning and mastery of physical skills and why?
(c) is it to improve cardio-vascular health, flexibility, strength and endurance? How important do teachers think this is? Should the children learn what happens to their bodies when they get hot?
(d) to help children learn social skills by being introduced to sharing, working co-operatively, and being able to

handle competition through physical activity;

(e) to promote active life styles, good habits, enjoyment of physical activity, a sense of achievement, well being, and a feeling of wanting to do more.

(iii) The process of physical education — the learning process of planning, performing and evaluating, the knowledge, skills and understanding they need to acquire, and the teaching process of selecting different strategies according to the intended outcomes, i.e. the different methods of approach teachers will need to employ with nursery children, reception, Year 1 and Year 2, including differentiation. This involves the setting of simple tasks, good powers of observation and identification, ability to provide feedback, evaluating, assessing and reporting procedures.

(iv) Entitlement — catering for all the individual needs of the children to ensure they all get equal opportunities to receive a balanced and constructive programme regardless of ability, learning difficulties, physical handicaps, different backgrounds, gender, race, etc.

(v) Resources — what resources have the school got in order to carry out this policy?

(vi) Safety:

(a) safety factors for teachers such as checking the apparatus, clothing, footwear, no jewellery etc.;

(b) the storage of apparatus and equipment to ensure ease of accessibility;

(c) rules concerning the handling of the apparatus;

(d) the layout of the apparatus to ensure progression;

(e) the organisation of getting out equipment and apparatus.

Overall planning

This is a general overview of each area of activity, i.e. games, gymnastic activities, dance and perhaps swimming. In the case of the nursery, it will be a statement on each category of movement education.

In order to justify the inclusion of each area of activity, it is necessary to state what the needs of the children are and how these needs will be met in the long term.

Statements under this heading should relate to the areas of activity outlined in the National Curriculum Physical Education Orders.

Games

Points to be considered are:

(i) Why include games in the PE programme? You will need to justify the playing of games in the PE programme and the nature and purpose of games in the early years.

(ii) What are the needs of the children in your school? Do these match up with the National Curriculum areas of activity — games for Key Stage 1?

(iii) How will you meet these needs — what resources do you have? Will the lessons take place out of doors in the playground, if so do you have any playground markings that will help?

(iv) How much time will be devoted to games? The *minimum* recommendation of time spent on physical education per year at Key Stage 1 is 36 hours. What proportion of the time allocation will be devoted to games? Will you spend more time out of doors in the summer?

Gymnastic activities

Points to be considered are:

(i) Why include gymnastic activities in the PE programme? You will need to define and justify gymnastic activities in the PE programme and the nature and purpose of gymnastic activities in the early years.

(ii) What are the needs of the children in your school? Do these match up with the National Curriculum areas of activity — gymnastic activities for Key Stage 1.

(iii) How will you meet these needs? Will the floor work and apparatus work be done in the same lesson? What resources do you have? Do you have a large hall? Is it shared by infant and junior classes? Do other activities take place in the hall, such as music lessons? Will the children be taught to put out the apparatus and learn to handle it correctly?

(iv) How much time will be devoted to gymnastic activities? See under games the point about the number of hours. Do you need more time than that allocated to dance and games because of putting out the large apparatus? Will you lose time in the autumn term for such activities as Christmas play rehearsals?

Dance

Points to be considered are:

(i) Why include dance in the PE programme? You will need to justify dance in the PE programme and the nature and purpose of dance in the early years.

(ii) What are the needs of the children in your school? Do these match up with the National Curriculum areas of activity — dance for Key Stage 1?

(iii) How will you meet these needs? What resources will you need such as, cassettes, amplification of the cassette player, percussion instruments, use of video?

(iv) How much time will be allocated to dance? See under games the point about the number of hours. Will you devote a block of time to dance to link with specific topic work? Will you plan one unit of work a year or more?

Swimming

Points to be considered are:

(i) Why include swimming in the PE programme? You will need to justify swimming in the PE programme and the nature and purpose of swimming in the early years.

(ii) What are the needs of the children in your school? Do these match up with the National Curriculum areas of activity — swimming, bearing in mind that children at Key stage 1 will follow the Key Stage 2 programme?

(iii) How will you meet these needs? Where will the swimming take place? What arrangements are made for transport, funding, supervision of the children?

(iv) How much time will be allocated for swimming? Can this be justified bearing in mind the other areas of activity to be covered? When will swimming take place? Will it be offered to all children or just those who have not yet learnt to swim?

Year group planning

Units of work

In order to get progression from one year to the next, teachers need to plan out what work they are going to cover. Each area of activity can be divided up into a series of themes. A theme will last about six sessions and is referred to as a unit of work. Built into these units is the new work to be covered. This will enable progression to be made, although it is accepted that in the early years much of the work needs to be repetitive, and opportunity given for the children to explore, experiment and practise what they are doing. However, unless some new work is introduced they will get bored and stale.

It is recommended that at Key Stage 1 a minimum of thirty-six hours a year is spent on physical education. This means that at least three twenty minute lessons can take place each week, i.e. one for each area of activity. This does not include getting changed and travelling to and from the hall or playground.

Time will have to be allowed for such activities as rehearsing for Christmas plays, and if swimming is taught then less time may be devoted to games, gymnastic activities and dance. **It is important that a balance between the areas of activity is maintained over the school year.**

Two aspects need to be given particular attention when planning units of work. One is the transference from the nursery to reception and the other mixed ages in a particular class.

Transference from nursery to reception

Units of work based on the areas of activity are not appropriate for the nursery because movement education spans all areas. What needs to be identified in the nursery are the different areas of experience outlined in chapter 2, in order to see that a balance of activities is maintained.

The transfer to the reception class may be gradual and children may well attend mornings only for a while, although some children in the class may be already attending full time. New children are often incorporated into the class during the year. The teacher will have to identify what she feels is important for her children and provide a basis on which the units of work for years one and two may be built.

Units of work could include body awareness, spatial awareness, stories in movement, introduction to games equipment, work on the large apparatus, and movement to music.

What is important is that differentiation is built into the work so that all the children can benefit.

Mixed age groups

Where there are two or possibly more different age groups in a class, there will have to be clear agreement between teachers on what work will be covered. Units of work can be repeated if appropriate.

All units of work should relate to the programmes of study and end of Key Stage Descriptions outlined in the National Curriculum.

Examples of units of work are given at the end of each chapter on games, gymnastics activities, dance and swimming.

Lesson plans

Once the outline of the work for the year is planned out then the teacher can plan each lesson in detail.

The format of a lesson is given in each relevant chapter.

Evaluation

At the end of each unit of work the teacher should evaluate its success. She needs to reflect on whether the children understood and were able to carry out the tasks, whether the level of work was demanding enough and whether the children enjoyed it.

By critical analysis, the teacher can identify what needs to be improved if necessary, and the units of work can be updated at the end of the school year ready for the next.

Assessment

All the time a teacher is working with her children she will be making judgments about individual progress. She gets immediate feedback by the nature of the subject.

Whereas this will be mostly a mental exercise, the time will come when she has to record her observations in order to produce written evidence of what the children have learnt, how they are progressing and any special help they may need. This calls for good observation skills and the ability to identify what is happening.

Criteria for assessment needs to be agreed as a whole-school policy and should be centred around the end of Key Stage Descriptions. Although not compulsory, an agreed method of assessing will make things simpler for the teacher.

An example of an assessment sheet is included at the end of this section.

Record keeping

Teachers need to keep records of the work they have covered in order to ensure progression and to keep a note of which pieces of apparatus a group is working on in gymnastics. Children can also keep simple records in the form of a diary which they write up after they have got changed perhaps. This can be in pictorial form if they are still struggling with their letters.

Reporting to parents

A brief statement of the child's progress should be included in the annual report to parents. This can be based on end of Key Stage Descriptions or on the learning outcomes identified in the units of work.

If any problems have been identified they need to be reported verbally to parents as a matter of urgency because medical advice may need to be sought.

An example of a simple assessment procedure that could be used by class teacher

PHYSICAL EDUCATION ASSESSMENT. KEY STAGE 1

NAME OF CHILD .... CLASS ....

AREA OF ACTIVITY ....

CRITERIA FOR ASSESSMENT (See National Curriculum)

....

....

E = EFFORT   A = ACHIEVEMENT

Tick the appropriate boxes	Very good A E		Fairly good A E		Needs help A E	
Answers the task						
Degree of physical skill						
Quality of movements						
Inventiveness/originality						
Concentration						
Ability to work with others						
Knowledge and understanding						

Comments

Signed .... Class teacher.   Date ....

Assessment sheet for physical education

Key Stage 1

How to use this sheet

(i) One sheet per child, to be kept in the child's portfolio.
(ii) This sheet can be used for any activity.
(iii) A statement from the National Curriculum should be selected as the criterium for the assessment.
(iv) There is no need to fill in the whole sheet. Inventiveness, for example, may not be relevant in swimming.
(v) Effort reflects how hard the child tries, regardless of ability.
(vi) Achievement: this records how successful the child is in fulfilling the selected statement (see (iii)).

Criteria for assessment

Points to look for:

(i) *Answers the task*:
 (a) The task should be sufficiently open-ended for all children to be able to achieve, for example, 'find a way of rolling'.
 (b) Does the child follow given instructions?
(ii) *Degrees of physical skill*:
 (a) i.e. a *learned* action such as catching a ball. How coordinated is he?
 (b) Can the child perform the skill competently?
 (c) Is he able to adapt the skill in different situations and using different equipment? for example, catch a ball whilst still? on the move?
(iii) *Quality of movements*:
 (a) Are the movements performed well? for example, does he show a good stretch whilst balancing? Is he well aware of what his body is doing?
 (b) Does he show a good starting and finishing position?
 (c) Is he aware of the space around him and use it well?
 (d) Are his movements pleasing to watch?
(iv) *Inventiveness/originality*:
 (a) Is he able to come up with ideas without help?
 (b) Has he a range of ideas?
 (c) Is he able to convey ideas through movement?
(v) *Concentration*:
 (a) Does he listen and focus on the task?
 (b) Does he get on with the task without distracting other children?
 (c) Can he practise independently and try to improve?
 (d) Can he remember a phrase of movements and get them in the right order?
(vi) *Ability to work with other children*:
 (a) Does he share equipment?
 (b) Does he work cooperatively with a partner?
 (c) Is he aware of other children around him and take turns?
(vii) *Knowledge and understanding*:
 (a) Can he explain what he has done and why?
 (b) Is he able to observe and comment on what other children have done?
 (c) Is he able to interpret a task through movement?

The role of the curriculum leader or coordinator for physical education

The role of the curriculum leader or coordinator for physical education will be much the same as for other curriculum areas but may vary from school to school depending on its size and facilities.

The nature of physical education makes coordinating the programme more difficult because the outcomes are physical rather than tangible,

To summarize therefore:

i.e. there is no visual evidence of what has taken place in a lesson after it is over. However, the more the teachers pull together and follow an accepted policy, the easier it becomes.

The curriculum leader will probably have responsibility for the equipment and this means making recommendations to the Headteacher for its purchase, seeing that it is stored safely and tidily, keeping an eye on its maintenance and checking it for wear and tear.

Agreeing a common policy

In order to get teachers to agree on a common policy and implement it, it is necessary to win their support. This can only be done by sympathetic and sensitive coercion. They need to feel they have part ownership of any written documentation; to be presented with a definitive document which they have not seen before will most likely commit that document to the cupboard and forgotten.

The curriculum leader, therefore, in consultation with the Headteacher, will need to hold a series of meetings in which the teachers together can:

(a) recognize the need to develop existing practice in response to National Curriculum orders, OFSTED inspections, general improvement in organization etc., and make a positive decision to pull together to achieve agreed aims;

(b) identify existing good practice and build on it where necessary by bridging the gaps between what is good and what needs to be done;

(c) draw up a plan of action so that change can be brought about realistically without undue pressure on overworked teachers;

(d) recognize areas of resistance and develop strategies to win teachers over, if necessary, without letting them feel threatened or vulnerable;

(e) plan ways of getting feedback and amending policies if necessary.

Implementing a common policy

Having agreed on a policy, some of the implementation can be immediate, for example the storage of the equipment. Some will be ongoing, such as developing strategies for handling the large apparatus, and some will involve long-term planning.

The curriculum leader may offer to help individual teachers by team teaching, taking demonstration lessons or observing lessons. This is a sensitive area and needs to be carefully thought out and timetabling restrictions will need to be overcome.

In-service sessions led by the curriculum leader or an invited consultant can be very successful. Teachers need to identify what they hope to gain from such a session and make it clear to the leader so that the time can be used profitably. A chance for discussion should be built into the day so that it is a sharing process. Anxieties such as safety factors should be voiced and strategies agreed to help allay fears. Planning and carrying out units of work requires cooperation from everybody and the curriculum leader needs to be involved by talking to individual teachers, showing interest in what they are doing and giving support in any way possible.

Time needs to be earmarked for reflection, evaluation and making changes where necessary.

The curriculum leader would benefit from consultation with other curriculum leaders at conferences, courses, or support groups. She should be aware of the activities that take place in feeder nurseries and plan accordingly so that the transfer between nursery and reception is smooth. Similarly she needs to consult with the later years' curriculum leaders so that she can prepare her children for the transfer to Year 3.

At all times consultation with the headteacher, school governors, parents and support staff will keep everyone informed.

Providing and maintaining resources

These fall into three categories:
- (a) large gymnastic apparatus;
- (b) small games' equipment;
- (c) cassette tapes, players, percussion instruments etc. for dance.

Large gymnastic apparatus

(i) This needs to be stable but light enough for children to carry and set in place.

(ii) It should be stored where it is easily accessible.

(iii) There should be a range of tables, planks, benches, poles, offering different heights, large areas to stand on and jump from, sloping surfaces, opportunities to climb and hang, swing and balance.

(iv) Mats should be non-slip, washable and easily lifted into place.

(v) All apparatus should be regularly checked.

(vi) Any defects should be reported and the piece of apparatus taken out of use.

Small games' equipment

(i) There should be a variety of balls, bats, quoits, beanbags and skipping ropes.

(ii) There needs to be a range of hoops, cones, skittles and markers.

(iii) The curriculum leader needs to consult various educational catalogues to see any new innovations which come onto the market but should not agree to purchase anything new without consultation with colleagues.

(iv) An agreed method of storage needs to be adopted.

Dance resources

(i) Music for dance needs to be catalogued and available for use. Cassettes for use with specific units of work could be labelled and stored in an agreed place.

(ii) Percussion instruments will most likely form part of the music resources and teachers ought to know the procedures for borrowing them.

(iii) Any other resources such as masks, and dressing-up clothes, which may be required for a specific unit of work, will probably be kept with the drama resources.

Swimming equipment

(i) Any equipment needs to be stored in a container that will not rot if it gets wet.

(ii) Arm bands should be checked regularly for punctures.

(iii) Floats should conform to current safety regulations; children have been known to choke on pieces of foam that have been chipped from floats and lie on the surface of the water.

(iv) There is a range of exciting, colourful equipment to assist beginners and teachers should consult educational catalogues.

Ways to assist with the implementation of a school PE policy

Large apparatus

(i) This must be stored near where it is to be used or teachers will not use it.

(ii) If it is placed around the room against the walls (allowing space for the children to get round in order to lift it) then it is easier to move.

(iii) Large clear labels should be put on the walls identifying the home of each piece.

(iv) Plans of apparatus for each unit of work could be drawn on card, laminated and kept in a special box in the hall. For Year 2 children plans for each apparatus station could be drawn on card and laminated. These could be given to the children to assist them in getting out their apparatus.

(v) Agreed methods of handling apparatus by the children, which is followed by all teachers will ensure continuity and make the task easier.

Small games' equipment

(i) Four plastic storage boxes, one of each colour, containing a range of games equipment of that colour could be kept in the games cupboard. The boxes should have large labels identifying the contents so that they can be easily checked by the children at the end of every lesson.

(ii) Simple games that the children can play could be printed on cards, laminated and kept in the games cupboard. These could be games made up by the children themselves. The children could borrow the cards at playtimes perhaps.

Dance resources

(i) Titles of music suitable for each unit of work could be cross-referenced to assist availability.

(ii) Videos and other cross-curricular materials should be cross-referenced.

General ideas

(i) Units of work could be printed on cards and laminated for easy reference.

(ii) An 'ideas' book could be kept in the staffroom for teachers to jot down what went well with their children, especially games for them to play and dance ideas.

(iii) A shelf in the staffroom could be kept for reference books, guidelines, cassettes, and videos, together with assessment sheets, progress records etc.

(iv) Sharing children's work — opportunities should be given for children to watch other classes from time to time, this could be during assembly if appropriate.

(v) Children's work could be captured on video and used as a teaching aid, shown to parents at a parents' evening and shown to the children themselves.

To summarize therefore:

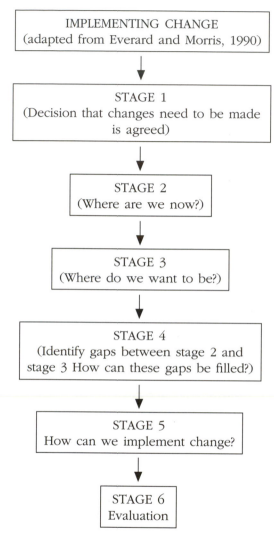

IMPLEMENTING CHANGE
(adapted from Everard and Morris, 1990)

STAGE 1
(Decision that changes need to be made is agreed)

STAGE 2
(Where are we now?)

STAGE 3
(Where do we want to be?)

STAGE 4
(Identify gaps between stage 2 and stage 3 How can these gaps be filled?)

STAGE 5
How can we implement change?

STAGE 6
Evaluation

Consultation necessary at all stages.
Imposed change is NOT effective
aim low — score high.

The inspection of physical education by OFSTED (Office for Standards in Education)

What the inspectors are looking for

Criteria specific to physical education (appropriate to age and ability):

(i)   Standards and quality — standards of achievement:

> 'Progress within the context of dance, games, gymnastic activities and swimming. All activities should be covered during Key Stage 1 although swimming could be confined to Key Stage 2.
>
>   Pupils should be able to:

Plan	— think ahead
	— imagine the finished action
	— anticipate responses from others
	— compose movements
	— devise tactics
perform	— with competence and versatility
	— select appropriate responses
	— produce good, relevant and original solutions
	— refine skills
evaluate	— observe and compare accurately
	— develop technical language
	— judge their own and others' performance by the quality of movement.

(ii)   Standards and quality — quality of learning:

> Taking into account pupils' ability to:
> — make progress in planning, performing and evaluating their movement in a variety of contexts

— practise, modify and consolidate skills

— explore, experiment, improvise their performance

— respond to instructions and more open-ended tasks

— perform as an individual and as part of a team, being cooperative and competitive

— work hard showing commitment to master a skill

— show concern for the safety of themselves and others.

(iii) Quality of teaching:

Physical and intellectual challenge which enables pupils to make progress to use their full potential.
Use of well-designed tasks to enable pupils to plan an activity, perform it successfully and evaluate that performance with clear criteria, including its effect on health.
Experience a balance of activities in lesson time.
Movement from dependence to finding ways of learning and improving fitness.

(iv) Resources for learning:

A range of equipment to cover the National Curriculum programmes of study.
Provision of sound equipment/video for dance.
Music tapes/CDs for dance.
Provision for transport for off-site activities.
All resources regularly checked and maintained.' (Adapted from Coventry Education Service 1993)

To summarize therefore, the inspectors will be looking at the standards achieved by the children, and the quality of teaching and learning. They will do this by watching lessons. They will want to see written evidence of which areas of PE have previously been covered and the planning for the future.

The inspectors will need a statement on equality of opportunity, including opportunities for children from different ethnic backgrounds, those with special needs, the more able children, and that gender issues are tackled.

Teachers should produce evidence of evaluation, assessment, record keeping and reporting to parents. This evidence will need to reflect good planning, and influence progress made by the children.

The report produced by the inspectors will cover such aspects as the quality of teaching, the quality and range of the curriculum, resources and their management, and links with parents.

Inspectors trained by OFSTED will have had five days' training and will be either, registered inspectors, team inspectors or lay inspectors. The registered inspectors will have had a further week's training as part of an HMI primary inspection team. They will have a range of professional and educational experience, except the lay inspectors who can come from any background other than teaching.

It is worth bearing in mind that the interests and welfare of pupils are seen as the first priority by all concerned.

In conclusion

Children have to be given the opportunity to progress at their own rate. They should all enjoy physical activity and no one can deny that they learn through doing. Unless they are offered a structured and developmental programme, they will miss out on so much and who are we to deprive them of the chance to run, jump, climb, swing, hang, play games, learn to swim and dance?

'One of the primary goals of education is to develop individuals to a point that they become happy, healthy, contributing members of society.' (Gallaghue, 1982)

References

BAALPE (1990) *Safe Practice in Physical Education*, Leeds, White Line Press.

BOTHAM, J. (in Adams) (1993) *Under Starter's Orders*, TES.

CAPLOW, T. (1964) *Principles of Organisation*, New York, Harcourt.

CASEY, E. (in Adams) (1993) *Under Starter's Orders*, TES.

COUSINEAU, W. J. and LUKE, M.D. (in Whitehead and Underwood) (1990) 'Relationships Between Teacher Expectations and Academic Learning in Sixth Grade Physical Education Basketball Classes', *Journal of Teaching in Physical Education*, New York.

CROSS, R. (1991) *Swimming and Teaching Coaching*, ASA Swimming and Teaching Enterprises, Loughborough, Leicestershire.

DES (1972) *Movement, Physical Education in the Primary Years*, HMSO.

DES (1989) *Physical Education from 5 to 16*, London, HMSO.

DES (1992) *Physical Education in the National Curriculum*, London, HMSO.

EVERARD, B. and MORRIS, G. (1990) *Effective School Management*, London, Paul Chapman.

GALLAGHUE, D. (1982) *Understanding Motor Development in Children*, New York, John Wiley & Sons Inc.

HARRISON, J. (1989) *Anyone Can Swim*, Loughborough, Leicestershire, Amateur Swimming Association.

HEATH, W. *et al.* (1994) *Physical Education Key Stage 1*, Cambridge, Stanley Thornes Ltd.

LABAN, R. (1947) *Effort*, London, MacDonald and Evans.

LEE, C. (in Cross) (1991) *Swimming and Teaching Coaching*, Loughborough, Leicestershire, ASA Swimming and Teaching Enterprises.

MANNERS, H. and CARROLL, M. (1991) *Gymnastics 4 to 7*, London, Falmer Press.

MAULDEN, E. and REDFERN, H. (1969) *Games Teaching: An Approach for the Primary School*, London, MacDonald and Evans.

OLIVOVA, V. (1984) *Sports and Games in the Ancient World*, London, Guild Publishing.

OPIE, I. (1969) *Children's Games in Street and Playground*, Milton Keynes, OUP.

RARICK, L. (1973) *Physical Activity*, New York, Academic Press.

ROSE, C. (in Williams) *Issues in Physical Education the Primary Year*, London, Falmer Press.

SACHS, C. (1937) *World History of the Dance*, New York, W.W. Norton & Co.

SCHOOL ASSESSMENT AND CURRICULUM AUTHORITY (1994) *Physical Education in the National Curriculum*, London, SCAA.

SLEAP, M. (1989) *Happy Heart Project*, London, Health Education Authority.

SLEAP, M. and WARBURTON, P. (1990) *Physical Activity Patterns of Primary School Children*, London, Health Education Authority, Interm Report.

SYLVA, K. and LUNDT, I. (1982) Child Development, Oxford, Blackwell.

TANNER, J. (1978) *Education and Physical Growth*, London, Hodder and Stoughton.

TITMAN, W. (1993) *Special Places Special People*, Credition, Devon, Southgate Publishers.

VYGOTSKY, L. (1962) *Thought and Language*, Cambridge, Cambridge University Press.

WHITEHALL, C. and UNDERWOOD, G. (1991) 'A Case Study of the Behaviour of Pupils of High and

Low Motor Ability in Primary School Games Lessons', *Bulletin of Physical Education*, BAALPE.

WICKSTROM, R. (1970) *Fundamental Motor Patterns*, Philadelphia, PA, Lea and Febiger.

WILLIAMS, A. (1989) *Issues in Physical Education for the Primary Years*, London, Falmer Press.

WIRHEAD, R. (1984), *Athletic Ability and the Anatomy of Motion*. Orebro, Sweden, Harpoon Publications.

Index

Index